Casanova's
Parrot

Casanova's
Parrot and

other tales of the
famous and their pets

Mark Bryant

BARNES & NOBLE BOOKS
NEW YORK

Published by MJF Books
Fine Communications
322 Eighth Avenue
New York, NY 10001

Casanova's Parrot
LC Control Number 2004105495
ISBN 1-56731-685-9

This edition published by arrangement with Carroll & Graf
Publishers, an imprint of Avalon Publishing Group Inc.

Manufactured in the United States of America on acid-free paper ∞

MJF Books and the MJF colophon are trademarks of Fine Creative
Media, Inc.

QM   10 9   8   7   6   5   4   3   2   1

Contents

Introduction

Mark Twain once said that 'A home without a cat, and a well-fed, well-petted and properly revered cat, may be a perfect home, perhaps, but how could it prove its title?' It is sometimes easy to forget that the celebrated figures from international history – whether poets, politicians, painters or princes – were all human beings with the same needs for food, drink, sleep and family life as the rest of us mere mortals. They too had homes to go to, books to read and pets to take for walks, lie on their beds and bring them comfort and entertainment.

The domestication of animals goes back at least to the Stone Age when Palaeolithic Man began to keep dogs. Horses appeared on the home front in about 3000 BC and cats and chickens entered the family fold soon after. From the beginning, far and away the most common indoor pets have been the dog and the cat but caged songbirds have also had a long history.

This book examines the pets of some 400 public figures, famous as well as infamous, from the 4th century BC to the present day, and covers celebrities from more than 20 countries across the world – from film stars, novelists and artists to kings, composers and explorers. Whether Nobel Peace prizewinners or fanatical dictators, flamboyant socialites or shy recluses all have kept pets throughout their lives. Sometimes, as tradition would have it, the pets and their owners had a lot in common – like Colette and her cats, or Sir Walter Scott and his dogs – but in other cases the kind of creatures invited into celebrities' homes were weird, wacky and bizarre beyond belief. Amongst these can be cited Charlie Chaplin's skunk, Edith Sitwell's puffin (with a wooden leg),

Baudelaire's bat, Dumas' vulture, de Nerval's lobster (which he took for walks on a lead), Ibsen's scorpion, Rosetti's wombat and Virgil's pet fly!

Pets have sometimes been treated by their owners as superior fashion accessories – the huge Persian cat which the novelist Elinor Glyn draped around her neck while giving a speech at a literary lunch at London's famous Dorchester Hotel in the 1930s being a rather literal case in point. Others have trained their animals to perform tricks – Adolf Hitler's dog could climb ladders and H.P.Lovecraft's cat played football – and Casanova even went so far as to teach his parrot to swear in French and sold it to a market trader to get revenge on an unfaithful mistress by shouting obscenities about her in the street.

Pets have also sometimes had a considerable effect – positive as well as negative – on the work of some of the greatest creative artists of the modern world. Scarlatti wrote music inspired by his cat walking over the keys of his harpsichord, John Steinbeck's dog ate half the first draft of one of this books (leading the author to think that it was probably not much good anyway), Dickens had a cat which used to snuff out the candle by whose light he was writing (no doubt to make sure he did not work too hard or strain his eyes) and Louis Wain only became a cat painter after he was given a kitten called Peter when he was 21.

Indeed such has been the esteem in which some pets have been held by their owners that the rewards for their companionship have on occasion known no bounds – Alexander the Great named towns after his horse Bucephalus and his dog Peritas, Frederick the Great erected monuments to his greyhounds and wanted to be buried with them, the Roman Emperor Caligula installed his horse in a marble stable and planned to make him a consul, and Louis XV had dogs which slept on velvet cushions and wore gold collars studded with diamonds. And many poets have composed verses to their pets, from Matthew Arnold, Thomas Hardy, John Greenleaf Whittier and Amy Lowell to Alexander Pope, William Cowper, Robert Burns and Lord Byron.

Pet names also have a fascinating history of their own. Some of Mark Twain's cats were called by such unusual names as Blatherskite, Appollinaris and Zoroaster in an attempt to help his young children pronounce difficult words. And as a deliberate insult to their human counterparts, George Orwell named his dog Marx, the political cartoonist David Low called his Musso (after Mussolini) and Dorothy Parker christened a particularly incontinent puppy after President Woodrow Wilson, because he was 'full of shit'. (She also had a canary called Onan – because it kept spilling its seed on the ground...) And one of Poet Laureate Robert Southey's many cats had one of the longest names ever: His Serene Highness, the Archduke Rumpelstilzchen, Marquis Macbum, Earl Tomlemange, Baron Raticide, Waouhler and Skaratsch – luckily it was a hearth-loving cat and did not need to be called in each night!

It has been a true delight to work on Casanova's Parrot and a great sadness to know that at some point the writing had to stop. However, I continue to collect anecdotes and information about pets of famous (and infamous) people from all periods of history and would welcome any further suggestions from readers for future editions. Meanwhile, it only remains for me to thank all those at Ebury Press who have been involved in the preparation of this book for producing such a handsome volume.

Mark Bryant
London, 2002

Casanova's
Parrot

Novelists

Sir Kingsley Amis (1922–95)

British novelist and poet. The author of *Lucky Jim* (1954) and the Booker Prize-winning *The Old Devils* (1986), among others – and the father of Martin Amis – Kingsley Amis owned cats and dogs throughout his life. His last cat was called Sarah Snow and features in the poem 'Cat English'.

J.M. Barrie (1860–1937)

British novelist and playwright. The author of *Peter Pan* (1904) and other works had a large black-and-white male Newfoundland dog called Luath which was the model for Nana in the play. In addition he had a brown-and-white male St Bernard called Porthos.

Charlotte Brontë (1816–55)

British novelist. The author of *Jane Eyre, Shirley* and *Villette* was the longest-surviving Brontë sister, and the only one to marry. She had a cat called Tiger and a black cat called Tom, who died in 1841 and who is mentioned in a letter to her friend Ellen Nussey: 'Alas, little black Tom is dead. Every cup, however sweet, has its drop of bitterness in it.' After her sisters died she looked after Emily's tawny bull mastiff Keeper (the model for Tartar, half-mastiff, half bulldog, in Charlotte's novel *Shirley*, 1849) and Anne's black-and-white spaniel, Flossy, which she had been given in 1843. Flossy eventually died aged 11. Keeper – whom Emily drew in 1838 when she was aged 19 – had been given to the girls' father, but only Emily could control him and when she died in 1848 he followed her coffin to the church and was let inside to sit at the family pew for the service.

Brigid Brophy (1929–95)

British novelist and critic. Perhaps best known for her novels such as *Hackenfeller's Ape* (1953), Brigid Brophy was also a keen animal lover and was Vice-President of the Anti-Vivisection League. Herself an owner of cats, in her book *Don't Never Forget* she recalled the remarkable power which her mother had over the creatures which would eat out of her hand almost anything she offered them, including fruit. And as she explained, this was not because they were the kind of cats that would normally eat such bizarre non-feline foodstuffs but rather they did so 'for the pure pleasure of sharing her diet.'

Frances Hodgson Burnett (1849–1924)

British-born children's novelist. Born in Manchester, Francis Hodgson emigrated to Tennessee, USA, in 1865 where she married and had her first book published in

1877. Famous for such works as *Little Lord Fauntleroy* (1886) and *The Secret Garden* (1909), she had two cats, Dora and Dick. Dick was exhibited at the first-ever cat show in New York.

Samuel Butler (1835–1902)

British novelist. The author or *Erewhon* (1872) and the posthumously published *The Way of All Flesh* (1903) was a keen cat lover but always insisted on recruiting his pets from strays he found in the street, especially around his home in Clifford's Inn in London. As he said in a letter to his sister:

> No, I will not have any Persian cat; it is undertaking too much responsibility. I must have a cat whom I find homeless, wandering about the court, and to whom, therefore, I am under no obligation. There is a Clifford's Inn euphemism about cats which the laundresses use quite gravely: they say people come to this place 'to lose their cats'. [...] Well this happens very frequently and I have already selected a dirty little drunken wretch of a kitten to be successor to my poor old cat.

It was Butler who said: 'They say that the test of literary power is whether a man can write an inscription. I say, "Can he name a kitten?"' He confessed that he could not. He also remarked, 'If you say "Hallelujah" to a cat, it will excite no fixed set of fibres in connection with any other set and the cat will exhibit none of the phenomena of consciousness. But if you say "Me-e-at", the cat will be there in a moment ...' One of his cats was called Purdoe.

Butler was also fond of dogs and said, 'The great pleasure of a dog is that you may make a fool of yourself with him and not only will he not scold you, but he will make a fool of himself too.'

Karel Capek (1890–1938)

Czech novelist and dramatist. Best known for his play *R.U.R* (1920) – which introduced the word 'robot' into the English language – Capek had a cat called Pudlenka, which appeared on his doorstep just as another of his cats, an Angora tom, had died from poison. She appears in 'The Immortal Cat' in his book *I Had a Dog and a Cat* (1940), and two of her many offspring were Pudlenka II, who was killed by a dog, and Pudlenka III. Capek also had an Airedale dog called Minda, which gave birth to eight Doberman puppies, and two other female dogs, Iris and Dashenka.

Truman Capote (1924–84)

US novelist. Truman Capote (whose real name was Truman Streckfus Persons) is perhaps best known for his novel *Breakfast at Tiffany's* (1958) – which was turned into an Oscar-winning film starring AUDREY HEPBURN – and *In Cold Blood* (1966), which was also turned into a successful film. When interviewed in 1958 in his house in Brooklyn Heights, New York, he owned a large bulldog with a white face called Bunky.

Barbara Cartland (1901–2000)

British novelist. By her first marriage, Barbara Cartland was the mother of Raine, Dowager Countess Spencer, stepmother of Diana, Princess of Wales. She was also one of the most prolific authors of all time, producing more than 600 books from 1923 (she earned a place in *The Guinness Book of Records* in 1983 for writing 26 books that year). Cartland specialised in romantic fiction and always dictated her books to her secretary between 1 p.m. and 3.30 p.m. while lying down on a sofa in the library at her house Camfield Place, Hertfordshire, with a white fur rug over her legs, a hot water bottle at her feet and three dogs beside her. She also owned a black Labrador and a white long-haired lapdog.

Her dog Tai Tai became one of the few dogs to be preserved for posterity in wax at Madame Tussaud's museum.

Louis-Ferdinand Céline (1894–1961)
French novelist. Céline's literary reputation rests on his autobiographical novel *Journey to the End of the Night* (1932) and other works. Having been a collaborator with the Vichy government during the Second World War, he was forced to flee Paris for Germany and Denmark. On his travels to Baden-Baden and elsewhere he and his wife Lili were never without their pet cat Bebert which they carried with them in a haversack.

Raymond Chandler (1888–1950)
US novelist. Best known for his 'private eye' novels such as *The Big Sleep* (1939) and *Farewell, My Lovely* (1940), Chandler had a black Persian cat called Taki who was 14 years old in 1945. It was originally named Take, a Japanese word meaning bamboo pronounced in two syllables but he tired of having to explain this all the time. Though a cat lover all his life (he once said he had nothing against dogs 'except that they need such a lot of entertaining') he none the less admitted that he had never quite been able to understand them. Chandler referred to Taki as his secretary, as she was always present when he was writing – usually sitting on papers he wanted to use or on a manuscript he wanted to revise. She would sometimes lean against his typewriter and

'talk' at him for up to ten minutes at a time or else would just sit 'quietly gazing out of the window from a corner of the desk as if to say, "The stuff you're doing is a waste of time, bud."'

The cat also had a curious habit in that, though she was extremely good at catching all sorts of creatures, she never killed anything but would always bring her trophies proudly into the house for Chandler to take away from her and release back into the wild. She had also had no interest at all in mice: 'Mice bore her, but she catches them if they insist and then I have to kill them.'

John Cheever (1912–82)

US novelist. Best known for his short stories and novels such as *The Wapshot Chronicle* which won a National Book Award in 1957, Cheever owned a number of dogs and an old black male cat with half a tail called Delmore Schwartz which he hated. Originally called Blackie, it had been a gift (in 1960) from a friend and had been previously owned by Elizabeth Pollet, the former wife of the poet Delmore Schwartz (1913–66). The cat was the model for the sinister black cat in *Bullet Park*.

G.K. Chesterton (1874–1936)

British novelist and journalist. Famous for his series of short stories featuring the detective priest Father Brown as well as many other books, Chesterton owned a small black dog called Winkle in 1910.

Dame Agatha Christie (1890–1976)

British novelist. The crime novelist and author of the long-running play, *The Mousetrap*, had a wire-haired terrier called Peter who was the model for Bob in *Dumb Witness*. Christie dedicated the book to the dog: 'To Dear Peter, most faithful of friends and dearest of companions. A dog in a thousand.' She also had a black Manchester terrier called Bingo who was the model for Hannibal, the dog detective, in *Postern of Fate*.

Colette (1873–1954)

French novelist. Colette was best known for her 'Claudine' series of novels and those featuring Chéri; another book, *Gigi* (1945) was made into a very successful film which won nine Oscars and featured Maurice Chevalier. Colette was very fond of cats and once said 'By associating with the cat, one only risks becoming richer.' At one stage the French writer had a 20-month-old wildcat from Chad called Bâ-Tou but eventually she sent it to a zoo in Rome.

Colette also owned a male angora cat called Kiki-la-Doucette and a French bulldog, Toby-Chien, who featured in her book *Dialogues de bêtes* (1904). Up to this point her husband Henri Gauthier-Villars (whose pseudonym was 'Willy') had signed all the books they had collaborated on (notably the 'Claudine' novels) with his name, but *Dialogues de bêtes* was the first of her books that was signed 'Colette Willy'.

Colette had a number of cats including Fanchette, Zwerg, La Chatte, Kapok, Kro, La Touteu, Minionne,

Muscat, Petiteu, Pinichette, Toune and (her last one) Chartreux. When Zwerg died she wrote to a friend: 'We ought only to allow ourselves to become attached to parrots and tortoises.'

Wilkie Collins (1824–89)
British novelist. The author of *The Woman in White* (1860) and *The Moonstone* (1868) was a great dog-lover. His favourite was a brown-and-white Scotch terrier called Tommie. Collins hated horses.

Joseph Conrad (1857–1924)

Polish-born novelist and short-story writer. Famous for such books as *Nostromo* (1904), *The Secret Agent* (1907) and *Heart of Darkness* (1902), Conrad's original name was Jozef Teodor Konrad Korzeniowski. When working as a sailor on the *Narcissus* (on which his 1897 book *The Nigger of the Narcissus* is based), he had a pet monkey. He also later owned a dog called Escamillo. By coincidence, one of his passengers when he was first mate on the clipper *Torrens* in the early 1890s was the novelist JOHN GALSWORTHY.

Charles Dickens (1812–70)

British novelist. A great lover of cats, Dickens always included them in his writings – no less than three in *Bleak House* alone, notably the savage Lady Jane who sat on Krook's shoulder. Dickens himself also owned a number of cats at his house in Gad's Hill, though for many years they were not allowed inside the house as he also kept birds. The exception was a white 'tom' called William, whom he was forced to rename Williamina when she had six kittens and insisted on bringing them into his study. Despite constant efforts to clear the feline brood out of his work area, their mother persisted in carrying them back in until in desperation he managed to deposit the bulk of the litter with friends, keeping only one kitten – apparently born deaf – which he called The Master's Cat. However, the great author's peace of mind was short-lived, for she soon learned a new trick all of her own – she would snuff out the candle Dickens was reading by with her paw! As his daughter Mamie recalled, one night Dickens was reading alone in the drawing-room at a small table on which a lighted candle was placed:

> Suddenly the candle went out. My father, who was much interested in his book, relighted the candle, stroked the cat, who was looking at him pathetically he noticed, and continued his reading. A few minutes later, as the light became dim, he looked up just in time to see puss deliberately put out the candle with his paw, and then look appealingly toward him. This second and unmistakable hint was not disregarded, and puss was given the petting he craved. Father was full of this anecdote when all met at breakfast the next morning.

Dickens also had a white spaniel called Snittle Timbery which was given to him in New York in 1842. Originally called Timber Doodle (the American name for a woodcock), Dickens thought his new name was 'more sonorous and expressive'. In addition he kept mastiffs and St Bernards, an eagle, a horse and a raven called Grip which inspired the famous poem 'The Raven' by EDGAR ALLAN POE.

Isak Dinesen (1885–1962)
Danish-born writer. While living in Kenya, Isak Dinesen (whose real name was Karen Blixen) kept a female bush-buck gazelle called Lulu which she described in her famous book *Out of Africa* (1937), later made into an Oscar-winning film starring Robert Redford and Meryl Streep. She also owned Scottish deerhounds who, despite their upbringing, seemed happy to let the local deer take their place in front of the fire in the cold months.

Alexandre Dumas (1802–70)
French novelist and playwright. The author of *The Three Musketeers* (1844–5) and other books had, among his many pets, a cat called Mysouff which seemed to possess telepathic powers. While working as a clerk to the Duke of Orléans he would set off each day at 9.30 a.m. accompanied by his cat up to a certain point. When he returned at 5.30 p.m. he would find the cat waiting for him at the same point. However, if Dumas was held up at the office, somehow the cat knew and would not wait. The telepathic cat's successor, the white Mysouff II, was a less reliable pet. One day with the help of three of the family's tame monkeys (each named after a literary critic), he broke into Dumas' aviary and ate all his rare

and valuable exotic birds. Once captured, the culprit was
solemnly 'tried' by Dumas and his friends, one of whom
voted to shoot him straight away! However, another said
the monkeys had egged him on and the sentence was
thus reduced:

> We left Mysouff gloating over the mangled remains of his
> feathered victims, and his capture presented little difficulty.
> By merely shutting the door of the aviary we had the culprit
> at the disposition of justice [...] Mysouff was declared guilty
> of complicity in the assassination of the doves and quails,
> also of the wrynecks, widow-birds, Indian sparrows, and
> other rare birds, but with extenuating circumstances. He
> was merely condemned to five years of incarceration with
> the apes.

He later also had a Scottish Pointer dog called Pritchard that lost a hind paw in a trap, and a vulture named Jugurtha that he bought in Tunis and tried to teach to talk. Other cats he owned included Le Docteur.

George Eliot (1819–80)

British novelist and journalist. Mary Ann Evans (her real name) was a keen animal lover and once said: 'Animals are such agreeable friends – they ask no questions, they pass no criticisms.' She herself kept a pug dog, called simply 'Pug', which was a gift from her publisher, John Blackwood, in 1859 after she remarked: 'I wish some nobleman would admire *Adam Bede* enough to send me a Pug.' Eliot described Pug as being 'without envy, hatred, or malice' unlike some of her human friends. When the dog died 18 months later, Blackwood sent her a china pug as a memento. She also owned a bull-terrier, Ben, and a dark brown spaniel called Dash.

F. Scott Fitzgerald (1896–1940)

US novelist. Fitzgerald became instantly famous at the age of 23 for his book *This Side of Paradise* and his other works included *The Great Gatsby* (1925) and *Tender is the Night* (1934). He owned a cat called Chopin.

Anatole France (1844–1922)

French novelist. France, who won the Nobel Prize for Literature in 1921, included his own cat, Hamilcar, in his first successful novel, *Le Crime de Sylvestre Bonnard* (1881). Every night when the cat felt it was time for France to go to bed he would knock the pen from his master's hand.

Paul Gallico (1897–1976)

US novelist. Gallico made his name with the sentimental novel *The Snow Goose* (1941), which was based on a true story of a wild goose which became a pet of the British naturalist PETER SCOTT. He also wrote the thriller *The Poseidon Adventure* (1969) which was later turned into an Oscar-winning film. Other books included *The Silent Miaow* and *Thomasina* (made into a movie, *The Three Lives of Thomasina*). Gallico had two cats, Chin and Chilla.

John Galsworthy (1867–1933)

British novelist. Galsworthy, who won the Nobel Prize for Literature in 1932, is perhaps best known for the six novels that form his sequence *The Forsyte Saga* (1906–28) – twice televised – and a number of plays. He owned many dogs but his favourite was a black spaniel called Chris, acquired in 1906, who was the model for John in Galsworthy's novel *Country House* (1907). When Chris died in 1911, Galsworthy's wife Ada had a visitation from him. Galsworthy wrote about him in *Memories* where he is described thus:

All through his life he flew a good deal in his sleep, fighting dogs and seeing ghosts, running after rabbits and thrown sticks; and to the last one never quite knew whether or no to rouse him when his four black feet began to jerk and quiver. His dreams were like our dreams, both good and bad; happy sometimes, sometimes tragic to weeping point ... He did not at all mind one's being absorbed in other humans; he seemed to enjoy the sounds of conversation lifting round him, and to know when they were sensible. He could not, for instance, stand actors or actresses giving readings of their parts ... and, having wandered a little to show his disapproval, he would go to the door and stare at it till it opened and let him out ... Music too, made him restless, inclined to sigh and to ask questions ... At one special Nocturne of Chopin's he always whimpered. He was, indeed, of rather Polish temperament – very gay when he was gay, dark and brooding when he was not.

By coincidence Galsworthy was once a passenger on a ship which had JOSEPH CONRAD as first mate.

David Garnett (1892–1981)
British novelist and critic. The son of Constance Garnett, the great translator of ANTON CHEKHOV and other Russian writers, and the publisher Edward Garnett who encouraged such writers as JOSEPH CONRAD, E.M. Forster and W.H. HUDSON, David Garnett is probably best remembered for his novel *Lady into Fox* (1922) and his correspondence with T.H. WHITE. He was also a great friend of SYLVIA TOWNSEND WARNER and often

mentioned his own cat Tiber in letters to her. His grandfather, Richard Garnett (1835–1906), who was Superintendent of the Reading Room at the British Museum, wrote a poem on his own cat, Marigold:

She moved through the garden in glory because
She had very long claws at the end of her paws.
Her neck was arched, her tail was high,
A green fire glared in her vivid eye;
And all the toms, though never so bold,
Quailed at the martial Marigold.

Ellen Glasgow (1873–1945)

US novelist. Ellen Glasgow, who won the 1942 Pulitzer Prize for her novel *In This Our Life* (1941), was very fond of her two male dogs Billy, a French poodle and Jeremy, a Sealyham terrier, and even sent them postcards when she was away (addressed to 'Mr Billy Bennet' and 'Mr Jeremy Glasgow'). Both of them died before her and were buried in her garden in Richmond, Virginia, but in her will she left instructions that they were to be exhumed at her death and their remains placed in her coffin.

Elinor Glyn (1864–1943)

British novelist. Elinor Glyn, best known for her infamous 1907 novel, *Three Weeks*, had two long-haired Persian cats, Zadig and Candide, named after Voltaire's fictional heroes. Once, at a literary lunch at the Dorchester Hotel in 1939 – where she was a guest speaker – she wore the huge Candide, asleep, around her neck as a fox-fur. As reported by Anthony Glyn in his memoir of his mother in 1955: 'During the speeches Candide would open a baleful and somewhat desiccating eye upon the speaker and then go to sleep again. "Great success!" commented Elinor in her diary.'

Sir Henry Rider Haggard (1856–1925)
British novelist. The author of *She* (1887) and *King Solomon's Mines* (1886) had a Pointer dog called Bob. One night Haggard had a dream in which the dog seemed to be saying that he was about to die. The next day they discovered that the dog had been run over by a train.

When living at Ditchingham House in Norfolk, Haggard had a 150-acre farm with pigs, horses, turkeys, Alderney cows and Norfolk red-poll cattle. He also had two dogs when interviewed there in 1892, notably Poacher whose mother was a famous lurcher (a poacher's dog) who was known all over the west of Norfolk. One night its owner set her on Haggard's gamekeeper and after some shooting the dog was captured and its owner charged with attempted murder. After the trial the dog was condemned to be shot but Haggard pleaded to keep the animal and her offspring became a devoted and faithful pet.

Thomas Hardy (1840–1928)

British novelist, poet and short-story writer. Thomas Hardy is best known for such rural novels as *Tess of the D'Urbervilles, Far From the Madding Crowd* and *Jude the Obscure*. He had a number of dogs, one of which, Moss was killed by a tramp. His wire-haired terrier, Wessex (the pet of his second wife, Florence), was notorious for attacking visitors, with the exception of T.E. LAWRENCE (it once tore the trousers of JOHN GALSWORTHY). Hardy loved the dog as it deterred callers – it featured in three poems and was very spoilt, walking on the table at meals. Wessex died in 1926 aged 13. The poems featuring him were 'A Popular Personage at Home', 'Why She Moved House' and 'Dead "Wessex", the Dog to the Household'.

Hardy also kept a number of cats at his house, Max Gate, near Dorchester, Dorset. However, they were very ill-starred – three were killed on the railway in 1901 and another suffered the same fate in 1904, giving rise to the poem 'Last Words to a Dumb Friend', which begins thus:

> Pet was never mourned as you
> Purrer of the spotless hue,
> Plumy tail, and wistful gaze
> While you humoured our queer ways,
> Or outshrilled your morning call
> Up the stairs and through the hall –
> Foot suspended in its fall –
> While expectant, you would stand
> Arched to meet the stroking hand;
> Till your way you chose to wend
> Yonder, to your tragic end.

His last cat, Cobby, a grey Persian with orange eyes, survived him.

In fact Hardy seemed to keep open house for cats. When a visitor called on him at teatime one afternoon in 1900 and asked if the cats were all his he replied:

> Oh dear, no. Some of them are, and some are cats who come regularly to have tea, and some are still other cats, not invited by us, but who seem to find out about this time of day that tea will be going.

In the grounds of Max Gate, Hardy built a pet cemetery where various cats and his dogs Moss and Wessex were buried. When Hardy himself died his heart was supposedly buried in Stinsford Churchyard, Dorset, but there is a story that his sister's cat stole it from the kitchen table.

Ernest Hemingway (1899–1961)

US novelist and short-story-writer. While living at the Finca Vigia in Cuba Hemingway kept about ten dogs, including the black springer spaniels Black Dog (male) and Negrita (female), as well as 30 cats – including Princesa, Thrusty, Bigotes, Alley Cat, Crazy Christian, Dillinger, Furhouse, Fatso, Friendless, Uncle Wolfie, Barbershop (Shopsky), Ecstasy, Spendthrift (or Spendy, originally named after Stephen Spender), F.Puss and Christopher Columbus (a tabby). In fact Hemingway had so many cats that he built a separate building, the Cat House, for them.

In 1953 he had a grey-and-black striped cat called Willie which was so badly injured in an accident that Hemingway shot it. Willie had been the favourite cat of their sons Patrick and Gregory and was a keen bird-hunter. Very distant with strangers to whom Hemingway's wife said he presented 'a conservative banker's mien, aloof and businesslike', he none the less allowed friends to pick him up and stroke his stomach.

Hemingway said that he liked cats for their 'absolute emotional honesty' and once observed that 'Dogs is trumps but cats is the longest suit we hold.' Black Dog (Blackie) was his favourite pet and lived with the Hemingways for 12 years. They originally acquired him when the dog followed Hemingway back from one of the bars the writer frequented in Ketchum, Idaho. He slept beneath Hemingway's bed and when enquiries proved that no one had lost him the Hemingways took Blackie back to Cuba with them but made sure that he lived outside the house so that the other animals would not object. Black Dog died in 1956.

Their favourite cat was Boise who was no 'mere carnivore' but had a wide-ranging taste in food and Mary Welsh Hemingway recorded that he ate fresh mangoes, cantaloupes, honeydew melons, chop suey, Mexican tacos 'with burning hot sauce', potato salad, raw onion, raw celery, leeks, cole slaw, sauerkraut, sunflower seeds, 'all pies and cakes', chili con carne, fresh apples ('although he prefers them in a pie') and cucumbers ('raw with salad dressing'). Yet despite this bizarre diet, 'He still jumps like a feather in the breeze.'

James Herriot (1916–95)

British novelist. The author of many best-selling books on vets – which were adapted into the long-running TV series *All Creatures Great and Small* – was in reality James Alfred Wright. He had a number of pets himself, including two dogs, Hector (a Jack Russell) and Dan – 'faithful companions of the daily round' – to which the book *Vets Might Fly* (1976) is dedicated. He also had a beagle called Sam and a Border terrier called Bodie.

Patricia Highsmith (1921–95)

US novelist. The famous crime writer whose first novel *Strangers on a Train* (1949) was adapted into Hitchcock's celebrated film of the same name, had a cat called Spider. She dedicated her book *The Glass Cell* (1965) to the cat and described him as 'born in Palisades, New York, now a resident of Positano, my cellmate for most of these pages'.

Victor Hugo (1802–85)

French novelist, poet and playwright. Famous for such novels as *The Hunchback of Notre Dame* (1831) and *Les Misérables* (1862), Hugo had a cat called Chanoine, which used to sit on its own red ottoman in his house in Paris. He also had a dog called Chougna and a cat called Gavroche.

Aldous Huxley (1894–1963)

British novelist. Grandson of the famous biologist T.H. Huxley, Aldous Huxley first came to fame with his country house satire, *Crome Yellow* (1921) but his most enduring work is *Brave New World* (1932). Huxley owned two Siamese cats and wrote an essay entitled 'Sermons on Cats' (in *Music at Night*, 1931) in which he declared that, 'If you want to be a psychological novelist and write about human beings, the best thing you can do is to keep a pair of cats.' He goes on:

> Yes, a pair of cats. Siamese by preference; for they are certainly the most 'human' of all the race of cats. Also the strangest, and, if not the most beautiful, certainly the most striking and fantastic. For what disquieting pale blue eyes stare out from the black velvet mask of their faces! Snow-white at birth, their bodies gradually darken to a rich mulatto colour. Their forepaws are gloved almost to the shoulder like the long black kid arms of Yvette Guilbert; over the hind legs are tightly drawn the black silk stockings with which Félicien Rops so perversely and indecently clothed his pearly nudes. Their tails, when they have tails – and I would always recommend the budding novelist to buy the tailed variety; for the tail, in cats, is the principal organ of emotional expression and a Manx cat is the equivalent of a dumb man – their tails are tapering black serpents endowed, even when the body lies in Sphinx-like repose, with a spasmodic and uneasy life of their own. And what strange voices they have! Sometimes like the complaining of small children; sometimes like the noise of lambs; sometimes like the agonized and furious howling of lost souls. Compared with these fantastic creatures, other

cats, however beautiful and engaging, are apt to seem a little insipid.

J.K. Huysmans (1848–1907)

French novelist. A well-known cat-lover, Huysmans – who is best known for his book *A Rebours* (1884; *Against Nature*, 1959) – included many in his books. *En Rade* features his own grey cat, Mouche, who had green eyes. However, the death scene in the book is based on the real-life demise of his favourite cat, Barre-en-Rouille, a red-and-black-striped tabby that used to catch bats.

Henry James (1843–1916)

US novelist. Best known for such novels as *Portrait of a Lady* (1881) and *The Ambassadors* (1903), Henry James moved to the UK in 1876, living in London and Rye, Sussex. He disliked cats but owned a number of dogs, including a dachshund called Tosca, and kept a canary in a cage in his drawing room in Rye.

James Jones (1921–77)

US novelist. James Jones is best known as the author of *From Here to Eternity* (1951), his first book, which won a National Book Award in the USA and was made into a film that won eight Oscars. When interviewed in 1967 in his rented apartment on the Ile de la Cité, Paris, he owned a Burmese cat called Hortense, who was expecting a litter of kittens that Jones hoped to sell at $150 each.

Jack Kerouac (1922–69)

US writer. Born Jean Louis Kerouac, he was best known for his autobiographical novel *On the Road* (1957) and for introducing the phrase the 'Beat Generation'. When interviewed at his home in Lowell, Massachusetts, in 1967 he had a cat named Tuffy and described his family as 'my paralyzed mother, and my wife, and the ever-present kitties'.

Rudyard Kipling (1865–1936)

British novelist and journalist. Kipling won the Nobel Prize for Literature in 1907 and was enormously success-ful in his day for his poetry and stories. Famed as the author of *The Jungle Book* (1894), *Kim* (1901) and other tales, he also wrote a book about Boots the dog, *Thy Servant a Dog* (1930) which was illustrated by the *Punch* cartoonist G.L. Stampa (1875–1951). Boots, a Black Aberdeen, who tells the story of his adventures with his friend Ravager, was a real dog who was actually owned by Stampa.

Eric Knight (1897–1943)

British novelist. Eric Knight is best known as the author of *Lassie Come Home* which was turned into a very successful film starring Elizabeth Taylor (1943) and a long-running TV series. The dog in the book was based on his own dog, a collie called Toots.

Pierre Loti (1850–1923)

French novelist. The author of *Madame Butterfly* – whose real name was Louis-Marie-Julien Viaud – was also well known for his love of cats. Loti lived with his mother and aunt and owned a black-and-white angora cat called Moumoutte Blanche. A naval officer by profession, after a journey to China Loti acquired another cat, Moumoutte Chinoise, and these two featured in his book *Lives of Two Cats*.

H.P. Lovecraft (1890–1937)

US writer. Best known for his science-fiction tales, H.P. Lovecraft also owned a black cat that ate roast chestnuts and, he believed, spoke in a language all of its own. This language, he held, had a variety of intonations, each of which had a different meaning, and even included 'a special "prr'p" for the smell of roasted chestnuts, on which he doted'. The cat also like to play football and if Lovecraft tossed a rubber ball at him would send it flying back in a flash by lying on the floor and kicking at it using all of his four feet at once.

Sir Compton Mackenzie (1883–1972)

British journalist and novelist. The author of *Sinister Street* (1913–14) and *Whisky Galore* (1947) was a great lover of cats and was for many years President of the Siamese Cat Club. Beverley Nichols (another well-known cat fan who called his pets by numbers) tells how he once visited Sir Compton on his remote island in the Hebrides and was amazed to discover four elderly Siamese cats sitting quietly on the kitchen range. After some coaxing he managed to get one of them to allow itself to be picked up and was surprised to feel the heat of its rear end which was considerably in excess of what a human could stand. Marvelling at the capacity of the creature to withstand such temperatures he carefully replaced the cat which, on being seated on the stove once more, began to purr happily 'like a kettle when you put it back on the gas ring'.

Three of Mackenzie's cats were called Tootoose, Pippo and Sylvia. He observed: 'Somebody once said that a dog looked up to a man as its superior, that a horse regarded a man as its equal, and that a cat looked down on him as its inferior.' Among Mackenzie's many writings was a book, *No Cats About the House*.

Olivia Manning (1911–80)

British novelist. Best known for her series of books 'The Balkan Trilogy' (1960–65), Olivia Manning was brought up with cats and as an adult became a great cat lover herself and even wrote a book about them, *Extraordinary Cats* (1967), and a poem 'Black Cat'. She was particularly fond of Siamese cats, the first one she owned being called Eebou. Eebou was originally named Owl because of the way she gazed at people with her blue eyes but as 'no one can comfortably call "Owl, Owl, Owl,"' she rechristened her Hibou (French for 'owl' – Siam, now Thailand, once having been a French possession) and this became 'Siamesed' into Eebou. Eebou's kittens were Butch and Faro. Other cats Manning owned were Lucca,

Fooff, Archie, the huge seal-point Siamese Choula – 'a lump of a cat with a perfect mask of dark mauve-grey and eyes of a very pure forget-me-not blue' and the brown Burmese Miou (originally Ngo Ah-miou) – whose coat was 'the colour of snuff; he had a seal-dark line down his spine and a seal-dark mask; his eyes were topaz'. Miou, whose dark paws had 'the feel of velvet' and whose touch had 'the delicacy of a feather' had a curiously gentle habit of patting Manning awake with his feet. In the morning, 'wanting to get the day started', he would give her face a brush with the fur round his pads and if she refused to wake would do so again until she succeeded: 'Each time is the merest breath of a touch, yet it is more efficient than an earthquake.' As soon as Manning got up, the cat would dash off, 'delighted by the promise of breakfast and the excitements of out-of-doors.'

Guy de Maupassant (1850–93)

French short-story writer and novelist. Maupassant is perhaps best known for his stories such as 'Boule de Suif' (1880) and the novel *Bel-Ami* (1885). He was also very fond of cats and always had at least one beside him. He wrote an essay 'Sur les Chats'.

Margaret Mitchell (1900–49)

US novelist. Margaret Mitchell wrote only one novel – *Gone with the Wind* (1936) – which won the Pulitzer Prize, sold more than 25 million copies, was translated into 30 languages and was famously turned into an

Oscar-winning film in 1939 starring VIVIEN LEIGH. She was brought up with a menagerie of animals as a child, her family owning horses, ponies, dogs, ducks, a cow, turtles and even two alligators. There were also lots of cats. One female was called Piedy and she was followed by Hypatia and Lowpatia (a male whom Margaret taught to stand up and salute with his right paw beside his ear, being rewarded with cantaloupe, his favourite food).

George Moore (1852–1933)

Irish novelist. The son of the owner of a racehorse stables – which forms the backdrop for his best known novel *Esther Waters* (1894) – Moore was very fond of horses. He also owned a large grey tomcat that took no interest in female cats and was completely chaste – and by all accounts was also rather dozy, as Moore later recalled:

> He never sought the she, but remained at home, a quiet, sober animal that did not drink milk, only water, and who, when thrown up to the ceiling, refrained from turning round, content to curl himself into a ball, convinced that my hands would receive him...

Moore was also very fond of the song of a local blackbird that came to his garden when he was living in Upper Ely Place, Dublin, and was very concerned that the neighbours' cat would kill it. Each morning he would write at an open window on the ground floor, listening to the bird, and if the cat came in to the garden he would throw stones at the unfortunate moggy. Eventually, so concerned was he for the bird's safety that he decided to set a trap for the cat. The story is told by W.B.YEATS in his book *Dramatis Personae* (1936) in which he says that he was passing through Dublin on his way to Coole Park, County Galway – home of Lady Gregory, and Yeats' summer home for nearly 20 years – when he met up with Moore who told him that he had now in fact set up a trap for the cat. Some time later Yeats returned to Dublin and bumped into Moore again who seemed to be very depressed. Yeats asked him what was the matter. Moore replied: "'Remember that trap?'– "Yes."– "Remember that bird?'–"Yes."– "I have caught the bird.'"

Dame Iris Murdoch (1919–99)
Irish-born novelist and philosopher. Author of the Booker Prize-winning novel *The Sea, the Sea* (1978), among other works. Iris Murdoch owned a cat called General Butchkin. She also had a blue-eyed Welsh sheepdog called Cloudy which was the model for the magic dog Anax in her novel *The Green Knight*.

George Orwell (1903–50)
British novelist and essayist. Orwell, whose real name was Eric Blair, is best known for such books as *Down and Out in Paris and London*, *Animal Farm* and *Nineteen Eighty-Four*. He kept a dog called Marx and when running the village shop in Wallington, near Baldock in Hertfordshire in 1936, had a pet goat called Muriel.

Edgar Allan Poe (1809–49)

US poet and short-story writer. Edgar Allan Poe was the author of the famous poem 'The Raven', which was inspired by the raven in CHARLES DICKENS' *Barnaby Rudge* (itself based on Dickens' pet raven, Grip) and such horror stories as 'The Fall of the House of Usher' and 'The Pit and the Pendulum', both of which were later filmed featuring Vincent Price. Poe had a large tortoiseshell cat called Caterina which inspired him to write the horror story 'The Black Cat'. When Poe's 24-year-old wife Virginia was dying of TB in 1847 (they had married in 1836 when she was only 13), Caterina curled up on the young woman's chest to keep her warm. After Virginia died that year Poe more or less stopped writing.

Barbara Pym (1913–80)

British novelist. Best known for such novels of middle-class English life as *Excellent Women* (1952) and *Quartet in Autumn* (1977), Barbara Pym had a black-and-white cat called Tom. His death in his sixteenth year at their home in West Oxfordshire is described in a letter from Pym to the poet Philip Larkin in 1976. The cat had been getting very thin and fragile for some time but just before she decided to take him to the vet's to be put down Tom died quietly on a copy of *The Times*. At the moment of death a bizarre thing happened, as Pym recorded in her letter: 'When he became cold the fleas left his body – I suppose that was how one knew he had really gone. I'd never seen that happen before.'

She also had a tortoiseshell called Minerva who liked to eat fried tomato skins and custard.

Charles Reade (1814–84)

British novelist, theatre manager and playwright. Charles Reade's best-known work was his long novel about the fifteenth century entitled *The Cloister and the Hearth* (1861) which was inspired by the story of the father of Erasmus. For many years Reade lived with the actress Mrs Laura Seymour at 2 Albert Terrace, Knightsbridge. Mrs Seymour owned a white spitz dog called Puff which appears in the portrait of Reade seated in his study by Charles Mercier, c. 1870. The painting also shows a cat with two kittens which were also owned by Reade and Mrs Seymour at this time.

Saki (1870–1916)

British short-story writer. Saki (whose real name was Hector Hugh Munro) was best known for his witty short stories such as Tobermory – a tale of a talking cat. When serving with the military police in Burma in 1893 he was given a pet lion cub and described it thus: 'My beast does not show any signs of getting morose; it sleeps on a shelf in its cage all day but comes out after dinner and plays the giddy goat all over the place.' Munro's great-uncle had been killed by a tiger while serving in India.

Dorothy L. Sayers (1893–1957)

British writer. Dorothy L. Sayers is best known for her detective stories featuring Lord Peter Wimsey such as *The Nine Tailors* (1934). She also had a white cat called Timothy which appeared in two poems by her: 'For Timothy, in the Incoherence' and 'War Cat'. In the latter poem the cat reproaches her for lack of food after working hard to catch mice in wartime, and berates Sayers' other pet, a parrot '... "who sits there/using bad language and devouring/parrot-seed at eight-and-sixpence a pound/without working for it."'

Paul Scott (1920–78)

British novelist. Paul Scott's fame rests with *The Jewel in the Crown* and three other novels based in India which form the 'Raj Quartet'. He also won the Booker Prize for *Staying On* in 1976. When living in Hampstead Garden Suburb, London, in the 1950s the Scotts owned eight cats: Minty and Sooty (both black), three tortoiseshells, Rota (a ginger tom named after the antiquarian bookseller) and Baron and Beauty (both Russian Blues).

Sir Walter Scott (1771–1832)

British novelist and poet. Famed for such poems as *The Lady of the Lake* and numerous historical novels such as *Waverley* (1814), *Ivanhoe* (1819) and *Woodstock* (1826), Scott was a great animal lover, notably of dogs but also of one cat in particular. Named after a German fairytale, Hinse of Hinsfeldt (or Hinsefield) was Sir Walter Scott's pet brindled tom, immortalised in a portrait of the great Scottish writer at work by Sir John Watson Gordon. However, what is not revealed from the demure expression of the cat as he sits quietly by a candle on his master's desk is that Hinse was the terror of the Scott household and ruled the family home – which included a number of dogs – with a rod of iron. Indeed, such was the power of the pugnacious old tom's steely paw that the writer's favourite hound – an enormous dog called Maida – would be reduced to a whimpering wreck whenever the cat blocked his passage.

In 'Abbotsford' the American writer Washington Irving described the cat after he had visited Scott's house:

The cat assumed a kind of ascendancy among the quadrupeds – sitting in state in Scott's arm-chair, and occasionally stationing himself on a chair beside the door, as if to review his subjects as they passed, giving each dog a cuff beside the ears as he went by. This clapper-clawing was always taken in good part; it appeared to be, in fact, a mere act of sovereignty on the part of grimalkin, to remind the others of their vassalage; which they acknowledged by the most perfect acquiescence. A general harmony prevailed between sovereign and subjects, and they would all sleep together in the sunshine.

However, even a mighty warrior like Hinse was only allowed nine lives, and finally met his Waterloo in 1827 when he took on another pet, Nimrod the bloodhound. Scott once said: 'Cats are a mysterious kind of folk. There is more passing in their minds than we are aware of.'

Maida, who was as big as a Shetland pony, was given him as a present by his friend Glengarry and was named in honour of the battle in which Glengarry's brother had led the 78th Highlanders to victory. One of Scott's favourite dogs, it often appears in portraits of him, to such an extent that the dog began to hate painters. According to Washington Irving, Maida was sketched so often 'that he would get up and go away with every sign of loathing when he saw an artist touch brush or paper'. However, as Scott himself recorded, despite his size Maida was:

perfectly gentle, good-natured and the darling of all the children. He is between the deer-greyhound and mastiff, with a

shaggy mane like a lion, and always sits beside me at dinner, his head as high as the back of my chair.

Maida was the model for Bevis in *Woodstock* (1826) and Roswal in *The Talisman* (1825). When HARRIET BEECHER STOWE visited Scott's house some time after Maida's death she saw a tomb to the dog near the front door of the house which featured a sculpture of Maida. Beneath it was an inscription in Latin which Stowe translated as follows:

At thy lord's door, in slumbers light and blest,
Maida, beneath this marble Maida rest.
Light lie the turf upon thy gentle breast.

Another favourite dog of Scott's was Camp, who was one of his first dogs and was his constant companion while writing *The Lay of the Last Minstrel* (1805). He appeared in two paintings of Scott by Sir Henry Raeburn and one by James Saxon, and by himself in a painting by Howe. According to Scott, Camp 'understood whatever was said to him'. On Camp's death Scott's friends wrote poems in Latin, French, Greek, Hebrew, German, Arabic and Hindi to his memory. In a letter to a friend from 1828 Scott describes the dog:

Camp was got by a black-and-tan English terrier ... out of a thoroughbred English brindled bull-bitch. He was of great strength and very handsome, extremely sagacious, faithful and affectionate to the human species, and possessed of a great turn for gayety and drollery ... His great fault was an

excessive ferocity towards his own species, which sometimes
brought his Master and himself into dangerous scrapes. He
used to accompany me always in coursing, of which he was a
great amateur, and was one of the best dogs for finding hares
I ever saw ...

When Camp died aged about 12 in 1809 he was buried in the garden of Scott's house in Castle Street, Edinburgh, opposite the window of the room in which Scott wrote.

Scott was very fond of dogs and always wrote with one by his side. Other dogs he owned included the grey-hounds Bran, Douglas and Hector (which used to lie beneath Scott's writing table gnawing at his shoelaces) and one called Percy which had a tomb erected to his memory in Scott's garden. Another greyhound was Hamlet, which was originally named Marmion but Scott rechristened him 'in honour of his inky coat'.

He also owned a dog called Finette, which Washington Irving described as 'a beautiful setter, with soft silken hair, long pendent ears and a mild eye – the parlour favourite'. In addition there were a number of terriers which he tended to name from items in a cruet set. Thus there was a small female called Spice which he described as 'a little, wise-looking rough-haired terrier', Mustard, Pepper, Catchup and Soyal. Another female called Ginger gave birth to four puppies in his study when Scott was working on his *Life of Bonaparte* (1827). Lady Scott's favourite dog was Ourisque (or Ourie for short). Scott also had a pony called Earwig and a horse that he named Lenore.

Isaac Bashevis Singer (1904–91)

Polish-born novelist. The Yiddish writer Isaac Bashevis Singer was born in Poland and became a US citizen in 1943, being awarded the Nobel Prize for Literature in 1978. He was very fond of birds and used to feed pigeons on his daily walks in New York. When interviewed in his Upper Broadway home in 1981 he had two pet parakeets that flew about the apartment uncaged.

Howard Spring (1889–1965)

British novelist. Howard Spring is best known for his novels *Oh Absalom* (1938) – later renamed *My Son, My Son* – and *Fame is the Spur* (1940). He owned a Siamese cat called Characters in Order of Appearance which was so named after the novel by Romilly Cavan in response to Cavan's own tribute to Springs in which he called his own Siamese cat Absalom. Pleasant though this mutual admiration may have been, Cavan obviously had the better name when it came to calling his cat in at night!

John Steinbeck (1902–68)

US novelist. John Steinbeck won the Nobel Prize for Literature in 1962 and is best known for *The Grapes of Wrath* (1939) – which won him a Pulitzer Prize in 1940 and was later made into an Oscar-winning film – *Tortilla Flat* (1935) and *Of Mice and Men* (1937). He was also was very keen on dogs and always had one as a companion. After the death in 1933 of Tillie (properly Tylie Eulenspiegel, whom he named after the prankster in a series of medieval German tales), he bought an Irish terrier puppy called Toby which ate half of the first draft of his novel *Of Mice and Men*. Steinbeck was naturally very angry at this apparently wanton act of destruction but on further reflection felt that perhaps the dog may have been acting critically and thus was not over-zealous in his recriminations and gave him only a modest spanking, rather than 'ruin a good dog for a manuscript I'm not sure is good at all'. Later, when the book was badly reviewed his suspicions were confirmed, and he promoted Toby to be 'lieutenant-colonel in charge of literature' adding that 'as for the unpredictable literary enthusiasms of this country, I have little faith in them.'

On his 10,000-mile tour of the USA in 1960, Steinbeck took with him a huge ten-year-old French poodle called Charley ('Actually his name is Charles le Chien'), who only responded to commands in French. The journey is described in his book, *Travels with Charley* (1963). Charley would sit in the passenger seat next to Steinbeck as they drove around and whenever the dog wished to get out of the car he used to lean across to the writer, put his nose close to his ear and say 'Ftt'. Steinbeck explained Charley's remarkable ability to pronounce the consonant F, the only dog he knew that could do this, by the fact that his front teeth were crooked: 'Because his upper front teeth slightly engage his lower lip Charley can pronounce F. The word "Ftt" usually means he would like to salute a bush or a tree.'

Robert Louis Stevenson (1850–94)

British novelist and short-story writer. Robert Louis Stevenson first achieved fame with *Treasure Island* (1883) which was quickly followed by *Kidnapped* (1886) and *The Strange Case of Dr Jekyll and Mr Hyde* (1886). Earlier in his career he bought a small female donkey called Modestine which he describes in his book *Travels with a Donkey in the Cévennes* (1879). Not much bigger than a dog and 'the colour of a mouse' he bought her in Le Monastier as he travelled south. When he reached St Jean du Gard, after 12 days and 120 miles, he sold her.

Harriet Beecher Stowe (1811–96)

US novelist. When she moved to Florida, the author of *Uncle Tom's Cabin* (1852) gave one of her cats, a large Maltese stray with a white underside called Calvin, to CHARLES DUDLEY WARNER, the editor of the Hartford Courant. When the cat died eight years later

Warner wrote a famous essay about him published in *My Summer in a Garden* (1882). The cat was buried in a candle box beneath the twin hawthorn trees in the Warners' garden (one white, one pink) in a spot he had been fond of lying in. Warner described Calvin thus:

> I think he was genuinely fond of birds, but, so far as I know, he usually confined himself to one a day; he never killed, as some sportsmen do, for the sake of killing, but only as civilised people do – from necessity. He was intimate with the flying squirrels who dwelt in the chestnut trees – too intimate, for almost every day in the summer he would bring in one, until he nearly discouraged them. He was, indeed, a superb hunter, and would have been a devastating one if his bump of destructiveness had not been offset by a bump of moderation. There was very little of the brutality of the lower animals about him; I don't think he enjoyed rats for themselves, but he knew his business, and for the first few months of his residence with us he waged an awful campaign against the horde, and after that his simple presence was sufficient to deter them from coming on the premises. Mice amused him, but he usually considered them too small game to be taken seriously: I have seen him play for an hour with a mouse, and then let it go with a royal condescension. In this whole matter of 'getting a living', Calvin was a great contrast to the rapacity of the age in which he lived.

Stowe also had a number of dogs that are described in *Our Dogs* (1862). These included a King Charles spaniel named Florence, who was acquired from Prince Demidoff in Florence; Carlo, 'a great, tawny-yellow mastiff as big as a calf, with great, clear, honest eyes, and stiff, wiry hair'; a Skye terrier called Ray and a Scotch terrier called Wix; and an Italian greyhound called Giglio, 'a fair, delicate creature, white as snow, except one mouse-coloured ear'. There was also a Newfoundland called Rover:

> He was grizzled black and white, and spotted on the sides in inky drops about the size of a shilling; his hair was long and silky, his ears beautifully fringed, and his tail long and feathery. His eyes were bright, soft, and full of expression; and a jollier, livelier, more loving creature never wore dog-skin.

Booth Tarkington (1869–1946)

US novelist. Best known as the author of the two Pulitzer Prize-winning books, *The Magnificent Ambersons* (1918, later made into a film by Orson Welles) and *Alice Adams* (1921), Tarkington had a French poodle called Gamin.

Mark Twain (1835–1910)

US novelist. Mark Twain, whose real name was Samuel Clemens, was best known as the author of *The Innocents Abroad* (1869), *The Adventures of Tom Sawyer* (1876) and *The Adventures of Huckleberry Finn* (1884). He also owned a number of cats, to four of which he deliberately gave very difficult names to teach his children to pronounce unusual words. They were called Apollinaris, Beelzebub, Blatherskite and Zoroaster. Others included Sour Mash, Buffalo Bill, Stan, Stray Kit, Danbury, Billiards, Babylon, Amanda, Annanci and Sindbad.

One of his cats, Tammany, had a kitten that liked to play billiards. He is described in one of Twain's letters:

> If I can find a photograph of my 'Tammany' and her kittens, I will enclose it in this. One of them likes to be crammed into a corner-pocket of the billiard-table – which he fits as snugly as does a finger in a glove – and then he watches the game (and obstructs it) by the hour, and spoils many a shot by putting out his paw and changing the direction of a passing ball. Whenever a ball is in his arms, or so close to him that it cannot be played upon without risk of hurting him, the player is privileged to remove it to any one of three spots that chances to be vacant.

Twain was very fond of cats – saying that 'They are the cleanest, cunningest, and most intelligent things I know, outside the girl you love, of course' – but disliked dogs because of the noise made by their barking. Unable to be without cats, he once rented two – Sackcloth and Ashes – when away from home. Twain once said: 'If man could

be crossed with the cat, it would improve man but deteriorate the cat.' He went on to add, 'A home without a cat, and a well-fed, well-petted and properly revered cat, may be a perfect home, perhaps, but how could it prove its title?' And his daughter Susy once said of her parents that, 'The difference between Mamma and Papa is that Mamma loves morals and Papa loves cats.'

Jules Verne (1828–1905)

French novelist and playwright. The author of *Around the World in 80 Days* (1873), *Journey to the Centre of the Earth* (1864) and other books had a large black dog when living at No.1 Rue Charles Dubois in Amiens near Calais in 1895. He also had a female spaniel called Follette and a dog called Satellite.

Sir Hugh Walpole (1884–1941)

English novelist. Best known for such books as *Rogue Herries* (1930) Walpole was a friend of VIRGINIA WOOLF and had a favourite dog – 'a ghastly mongrel' – called Jacob which he rescued from abuse by its owner as a puppy and which lived with him for 10 years in Polperro, Cornwall. It appeared as Hamlet in the three 'Jeremy' novels (from *Jeremy*, 1919). Interviewed in *John O'London's Weekly*, Walpole said he had owned many dogs, but admitted that none of them had ever approached Hamlet 'for wisdom, conceit, self-reliance and true affection'. In addition, 'he had Character, he had Heart' and 'an unconquerable zest for life'.

Sylvia Townsend Warner (1893–1978)

British novelist and poet. The author of *Lolly Willowes* (1926) was also a historian of early church music. While she was living at Frankfort Manor, Norfolk, in 1934, a sudden illness killed four of her cats. Another, Meep, was saved by moving her away and she subsequently gave birth to grey kittens before moving back to the Manor.

Warner was also a friend of and regular correspondent with the novelist DAVID GARNETT and they frequently wrote letters to each other about their cats. In one exchange she mentioned a curious incident concerning her dark grey cat, Tom, which slept on her bed:

> One evening I was reading in bed when I became aware that Tom was staring at me. I put down my book, said nothing, watched. Slowly, with a look of intense concentration, he got up and advanced on me, like Tarquin with ravishing strides, poised himself, put out a front paw, and stroked my cheek as I used to stroke his chops. A human caress from a cat. I felt very meagre and ill-educated that I could not purr.

H.G. Wells (1866–1946)

British novelist. The author of *The Time Machine* (1895), *The Invisible Man* (1897) and *The War of the Worlds* (1898), among many other works, had a cat called Mr Peter Wells, who was known to friends as Mr Peter. Allegedly when guests talked too loudly or for too long he would jump down from his seat and head for the door.

Antonia White (1899–1979)

British novelist. Antonia White, who was married to Tom Hopkinson, editor of *Picture Post*, and was the author of *Frost in May* (1933) and other works, was very fond of her female cat Domina. Her daughter Lyndall P. Hopkinson described Domina rather unkindly as an 'over-fed cat who had never been out of doors – except for the time she fell out of the window'.

T.H. White (1906–64)

British novelist. The author of *The Once and Future King* was given an Irish setter bitch called Brownie in 1933 after she kept sleeping on his bed when he was staying at an inn whose owner bred Irish setters. When she died in Ireland in 1944 aged 14, White was inconsolable and visited her grave twice a day and regularly wrote about her in his journal. In a desperate effort to distract him from the much-lamented Brownie, White's friend DAVID GARNETT advised him to get another dog. In consequence White went to Dublin where he bought another female Irish setter, which he named Killie ('she is called Cill Dara Something-or-other of Palmerston, but prefers to be called Killie, for lucidity', *Letters*, December 1944). This seemed to do the trick and Killie herself eventually died in 1958.

Sir Angus Wilson (1913–91)

British novelist. Perhaps best known for his bestselling novels *Hemlock and After* (1952) and *Anglo-Saxon Attitudes* (1956), Angus Wilson also owned a number of cats, his last being called Cookie.

P.G. Wodehouse (1881–1975)

British novelist. P.G. Wodehouse is best known as the author of numerous country-house comedies featuring the upper-class twit Bertie Wooster and his long-suffering butler Jeeves. A keen dog-lover, Wodehouse owned two Pekinese dogs, Winks and Boo, when he was captured by the Germans in Le Touquet, France during the Second World War. Indeed, it is alleged that the reason he was captured at all when France fell was because of British quarantine laws which would have forced him to leave the animals in France. Two other Pekinese dogs owned by him were Wonder and Squeaky. He also kept a foxhound called Bill and a cat called Poona. However, he does not seem to have been fond of cats for he once said, 'The real objection to the great majority of cats is their insufferable air of superiority.' This is born out in his famous short-story 'The Story of Webster'.

Virginia Woolf (1882–1941)

British novelist. Virginia Woolf's best known works include *Mrs Dalloway* (1925) and *To the Lighthouse* (1927). One of her lesser works is *Flush* (1933) the fictional 'biography' of the famous spaniel owned by ELIZABETH BARRETT BROWNING. She and her husband Leonard owned a female marmoset called Mitz who is described in Leonard's autobiography *Downhill All the Way* (1967). A gift from Victor Rothschild, when Rothschild was living in Cambridge, Mitz was very fond of honey but ate almost anything from mealworms and fruit to lizards and sparrows and had a special passion for macaroons and tapioca pudding which she seized in both hands and stuffed into her mouth 'so full that large blobs of tapioca oozed out at both sides of her face'. Mitz went everywhere with Leonard, either squeezed inside his waistcoat or perched on his shoulder. In the evenings, the moment it became dark Mitz would leave Leonard and curl herself up into a ball in a large birdcage in his room which he kept full of scraps of silk. As soon as the sun rose the following day she would leave the cage and return to his side.

When out driving in their open-topped car Mitz would always sit on Leonard's shoulder and when motoring through Germany in the 1930s often received Nazi salutes from bemused soldiers and uniformed officials. The Woolfs kept Mitz for five years but she eventually died of the cold one winter at their home, Monk's House, Rodmell.

They also had a dog named Sally, a blonde cocker spaniel bitch called Pinka – which was a present to Virginia from her close friend VITA SACKVILLE-WEST – and a cat called Potto.

Emile Zola (1840–1902)
French novelist. Best known for such books as *Nana* (1880), and *Germinal* (1885), Emile Zola owned a Labrador dog called Bertrand.

Royalty

Alexander III (356–323 BC)

King of Macedonia. Alexander III, better known as Alexander the Great and one of the most successful empire builders in ancient history, conducted his campaigns mounted on a wild black stallion. Alexander's father, Philip of Macedonia, had bought the horse in about 346 BC but had been unable to tame it. However, the ten-year-old Alexander noticed that the horse was frightened of its own shadow and so turned him to face the sun, thus eliminating his shadow. The moment the horse was calm Alexander leapt on his back and began to train him. Part of this training included making the horse kneel in full harness so that Alexander could mount him when he was wearing heavy armour. The horse lived a long time and had been ridden for 11,000 miles in eight years by the time Alexander reached India in 326 BC. Bucephalus eventually died at the age of 30 during the final battle against Rajah Porus on the River Jhelum. Alexander named the town of Bucephala in his honour (now Jhelum in Pakistan).

The name Bucephalus means 'ox-head' and in battle the horse was decorated with golden horns, which allegedly gave rise to the myth of the unicorn.

Alexander also had a favourite dog, Peritas, and named a town after him. A monument to the dog was erected in the town's main square. Alexander was reputedly a cat-hater.

Alexander III (1845–94)

Tsar of Russia. The son of Alexander II, who had been assassinated by revolutionaries, and the father of the last

Tsar of Russia, NICHOLAS II (who suffered a similar fate), Alexander III was lucky to die of natural causes – especially as there had been a number of attempts on his own life. He was a great dog-lover whose sheepdog Kamchatka was killed when the imperial train was blown up by revolutionaries at Borki in 1888. His daughter, the duchess of Saxe-Coburg, was also fond of dogs and at one time owned six including a retriever called Caesar and a Skye terrier which was a particular favourite.

Anne (1665–1714)

Queen of Great Britain and Ireland. Queen Anne, who was the daughter of JAMES II and sister of WILLIAM III's wife Mary, is the queen in the children's rhyme 'Pussy cat, pussy cat, where have you been?' She enjoyed hunting and had a specially made open chaise pulled by a single black horse which she drove furiously in stag-hunts in Windsor Forest. The founder of Royal Ascot, her winning racehorses included Star which won at York on 30 July 1714, but she never heard the result as she died the next day.

Anne Boleyn (*c.* 1507–35)

English queen. The second wife of HENRY VIII and former intimate of the poet SIR THOMAS WYATT among others, Anne Boleyn owned a French lapdog she called 'Little Purkoy' and a greyhound named Urian. She also owned horses. Her ghost reputedly still haunts her family home of Blicking Hall, Norfolk. Every 19 May (the day of her execution in the Tower of London) her spectre allegedly still appears on the estate, sitting with her severed head cradled on her knees, in a coach drawn by four headless horses and driven by a headless coachman. However, there is no mention of her having a headless dog on her lap as well.

Princess Marie Bonaparte (1882–1962)

French princess. The granddaughter of NAPOLEON's brother Lucien, Princess Marie Bonaparte (otherwise known as Princess George of Greece), had a chow dog called Topsy about which she wrote a book. This was subsequently translated from French into German by the famous psychiatrist SIGMUND FREUD, who was a close friend and whom she had helped to get out of Austria when the Nazis began to round up Jews. The last of the Bonaparte line was Jerome Napoleon Bonaparte who died in 1945 after tripping over his dog's lead.

Julius Caesar (c. 101–44 BC)

Roman emperor. A good horseman, Caesar's favourite horse had hoofs that were more like human feet and later had its own statue. As the Roman historian Suetonius recorded:

> This charger of his, an extraordinary animal with feet that looked almost human – each of its hoofs was cloven in five parts, resembling human toes – had been foaled on his private estate. When the soothsayers pronounced that his

master would one day rule the world, Caesar carefully reared, and was the first to ride, the beast; nor would it allow anyone else to do so. Eventually he raised a statue to it before the Temple of Mother Venus.

He also reputedly owned a giraffe.

Caligula (AD 12–41) Roman emperor. The favourite horse of this mad Roman emperor (Rome's third, ruling AD 37–41)) was called Incitatus and lived in a marble stable with an ivory stall and purple blankets and wore a jewelled collar. He was also given his own house to live in, complete with furniture and slaves. Caligula even planned to make him a consul.

Catherine the Great (1729–96)
Empress of Russia. It might be expected that Catherine the Great, who was born Sophia Augusta Frederica von Anhalt-Zerbst in Stettin, Pomerania, Prussia, of German parents would own Pomeranian dogs. However, there is

no evidence to support this. She was certainly given two English greyhounds by her English physician, Dr Dimsdale, the female of which gave birth to her first litter in Catherine's imperial state bedroom. In addition she had a black spaniel. When it died she had it stuffed and buried in a pyramid-shaped tomb.

Notorious for her extramarital affairs, Catherine was reputedly secretly married to the one-eyed cavalry officer Gregory Potemkin in 1774, who gave her a kitten. She was also very fond of horses, but the rumour that she died after being crushed while having sex with one is untrue. One animal whose life she obviously held in some contempt was the ermine – her coronation robes were made of no less than 4000 of their skins.

Charlemagne (742–814)
King of the Franks and Holy Roman Emperor. The King of the Persians and Caliph of Baghdad, Harun al-Rachid, presented Charlemagne with an elephant called Abu al-Abbas. Charlemagne kept the animal in his capital, Aix-la-Chapelle. His own favourite charger was called Blanchard.

Charles I (1600–49)
King of England, Wales and Scotland. King Charles was very fond of dogs and commissioned Van Dyck to paint a picture of five of his children with their dogs, a small Blenheim Cavalier Spaniel in the foreground and a large mastiff in the centre on which the Prince of Wales rested his hand. One of his dogs was a spaniel called Rogue

which was reputed to have accompanied the king as he walked to his execution on 30 January 1649. He also had a lucky black cat which died the day before he was arrested by Parliamentary forces.

Charles II (1630–85)

King of Great Britain and Ireland. 'Old Rowley', as Charles was dubbed by satirists, was so-named after his favourite Arab racehorse which often appeared at Newmarket races. Part of the course is still called the Rowley Mile. Charles kept many horses and fed them on bread and eggs. Another favourite horse was Flatfoot.

He also famously kept 'King Charles' spaniels (then liver-and-white coloured, not black-and-tan). These lived in his bedchamber which, according to the diarist JOHN EVELYN, 'rendred it very offensive, and indeede made the whole Court nasty and stinking'. The king even took the dogs to Council meetings. SAMUEL PEPYS also commented on Charles' pets, saying that when he visited the court, 'All I observed was the silliness of the King, playing with his dogs all the while and not minding his business.' One of his favourite dogs was called Cupid.

Charles V (1338-80)

Holy Roman Emperor. Born in Ghent, Belgium, Charles was joint ruler of Spain with his mother before being elected Holy Roman Emperor, ruling over Germany, Burgundy and northern Italy (the title was abandoned in 1806 – as someone once said, it was neither holy, Roman, nor an empire). His portrait by Titian (1536) also features his Irish wolfhound, Sampere.

Charles VIII (1470–98)

King of France. Charles, who was the only son of LOUIS XI of France and Charlotte of Savoy, reigned from 1483 until his death. He had a one-eyed black horse called Savoy which was named after the Duke of Savoy, who had given it to him as a present.

Charles IX (1550–74)

King of France. Responsible for the massacre of 50,000 Huguenots (French Protestants) on St Bartholomew's Day (24 August) in 1572 and totally dominated by his mother Catherine de Medici, Charles none the less took great care of his 36 miniature greyhounds which all wore matching red and green velvet collars. One of his greyhounds, Courte, featured in a poem by the famous Renaissance poet Ronsard. As Ronsard was deaf he was probably unaware of the barking protests of the other 35 dogs who no doubt also wished to be immortalised in verse... Courte was greatly indulged by Charles and sat at the king's table where he personally fed it biscuits and marzipan from his own hand. When the dog died he had its skin made into a pair of gloves which he always wore when out hunting.

Charles XII (1682–1718)

King of Sweden. A great general when Sweden was a major European military power, Charles defeated the Russians and dethroned the King of Poland before being killed in battle. He also owned a number of cats and had a favourite dog, Pompe, who died in 1703.

Cleopatra (68–30 BC)

Queen of Egypt. Cleopatra is alleged to have had a cat named Charmian and it is said that the mistress of Julius Caesar and Mark Antony copied the style of the cat's eyes in her make-up. Cats were revered in ancient Egypt and were even mummified after their deaths. Indeed Bast, the cat goddess was a major Egyptian deity who was a companion of the sun god Ra. The town of Bubastis was devoted to the goddess and every spring thousands of people would visit her 60-foot-high shrine. It is even said that the modern word 'puss' derives from 'pasht', a variant of the cat-goddess's name.

Edward II (1284–1327)

King of England. The king who lost to the Scottish under Robert the Bruce at Bannockburn and died a horrific death involving a red-hot poker at Berkeley Castle was a good horseman who was devoted to his horses and his hounds. He always took a lion with him on his travels.

Edward III (1312–77)

King of England. The father of the Black Prince and the instigator of the Hundred Years War with France by making a claim to that country's throne, Edward was a very keen hunter with hounds. Indeed it is said that before the famous battle of Crecy (1346), at which he defeated the French in a great victory, he took '300 couple of hounds and a hundred falcons' with him.

Edward VII (1841–1910)

King of the United Kingdom. Edward was fond of dogs and was patron of the Kennel Club, exhibiting dogs at shows himself. His first-ever dog was a retriever called Duck which was given to him by his mother QUEEN VICTORIA as an 11th birthday present but sadly died only a few years later, in 1854.

In later life, his favourite dog was a French toy bulldog called Peter who was run over on the eve of his coronation in 1901. Peter was replaced by a little terrier called Jack which went everywhere with him around the world – totally ignoring recently introduced European quarantine regulations. When Jack died in 1903 Edward had some of his hair made into a bracelet. His next, and last, favourite was the famous white wire-haired fox-terrier Caesar (which had a collar inscribed 'I am Caesar, the King's dog') who slept in a chair by the king's bed. When Edward died in May 1910 Caesar followed his master's coffin in the funeral procession.

Other dogs owned by Edward and his wife Queen Alexandra (1844–1925) included the Pomeranians Fozzy (which accompanied Edward to India in 1875) and Beaty (the gift of TSAR NICHOLAS II of Russia). Another gift was a Russian Samoyed from PRINCE OTTO VON BISMARCK in 1866, and in 1893 Tsar Nicholas gave two Borzois to Queen Alexandra, one of whom was called Alix whose hair she had spun into wool. In addition they had a collie called Rover, a pug named Puggy, Tom the poodle, a chow called Plumpy and a Siberian sheepdog named Luska. In addition, favourite pets of Queen Alexandra were a black-and-white chin (Japanese spaniel) named Punch, another called Haru and a pekinese called Little Billie. Alexandra was so found of her chin Togo – a personal gift from the Empress of Japan – that when it died in 1914 she erected a tomb to its memory at Marlborough House, London, which included a photograph of her with the dog. Many of the royal dogs were modelled by Fabergé.

In addition Edward inherited two blue Persian cats, Flypie and White Heather, when Queen Victoria died in 1901.

Edward was also very fond of horses and often raced them, such as Minoru who in 1909 became the only one of his horses to win the Derby while he was king. He had also won twice before (as Prince of Wales) with Persimmon and Diamond Jubilee, and a famous picture was painted of Edward and Persimmon after the Derby by S. Begg in 1896. Persimmon went on to win the St Leger, Astor Cup and Eclipse Stakes in 1897 before being put out to stud, and a bronze statue of him still stands at the Royal Sandringham Stud Farm. When Prince of Wales Edward's horse Anne Bush II won the Grand National.

When Edward died in 1910 his favourite horse was part of the procession with a pair of the king's boots reversed in the stirrups.

Edward VIII (1894–1972)

King of Great Britain (later Duke of Windsor). When Prince of Wales Edward was a keen horseman and rode point-to-point and steeplechase races. His mounts included Pet Dog, Rifle Grenade, Miss Muffet II and (in India) Bombay Duck. However, he gave up on the advice of Prime Minister Ramsay MacDonald after a bad fall in a race in Berkshire left him unconscious for half an hour and in bed for a month.

He also had a number of cairn terriers including Slipper and Pookie – he gave Slipper to Wallis Simpson as a Christmas present in 1934 but the dog ominously died when it was bitten by a viper in the garden of their home, Château de Candé in France, shortly before their wedding in 1937. Another favourite cairn terrier was Cora and when she got too old and infirm to jump up on his bed he had steps built to help her. In addition she was given a special pair of spectacles to counter the effects of altitude when flying with Edward on his travels.

As Duke of Windsor, after his abdication, he owned a succession of nine Windsor pugs, including Preezie and Dizzy (Disraeli). His pug Black Diamond was lying on his bed when the Duke died in 1972. Some of his dogs also had silver-plated dog-bowls.

Elizabeth I (1533–1603)

Queen of England, Wales and Ireland. The Virgin Queen kept a greyhound kennels on the Isle of Dogs (hence the name) and introduced the death penalty for anyone who kept greyhounds but was not a gentleman. However, that she was evidently not fond of cats is demonstrated by the fact that at her coronation a figure of the Pope made of wicker and filled with live cats was burnt as part of the ceremony.

Elizabeth's favourite, Robert Dudley, Earl of Leicester, owned an Irish wolfhound called Boye which features in one of his portraits (painted *c.* 1564).

Elizabeth, the Queen Mother (1900–2002)

Queen Consort. The wife of GEORGE VI, and mother of Queen Elizabeth II, Queen Elizabeth the Queen Mother was a keen animal lover. Apart from the corgis that she and George introduced to the royal residences she also had a Tibetan lion dog when living at Royal Lodge, Windsor Great Park. The Queen Mother was very keen on horseracing and became effectively the 'patron saint of racing over fences and hurdles' (*Sunday Telegraph* obituary) when she became a Patron of the National Hunt Committee in 1954. Her stables produced nearly 400 royal winners from her first horse Monaveen which won the Queen Elizabeth Chase at Hurst Park. Notable among these was Devon Loch, ridden by Dick Francis, which mysteriously collapsed only yards from the finishing post when leading the field in the 1956 Grand National. Her own great favourite horse was The Rip.

She also kept a herd of Aberdeen Angus cattle and a flock of North Country cheviot sheep at her castle at Mey in Scotland.

Franz Joseph (1830–1916)

Emperor of Austria and King of Hungary. After the assassination of his nephew Crown Prince Franz Ferdinand in Sarajevo, Bosnia, by a Serbian nationalist, Franz Joseph attacked Serbia, thereby starting the First World War. When living at Schönbrunn Palace, Vienna, his wife Elizabeth, who was murdered in 1898, owned a number of dogs including Newfoundlands, St Bernards and Great Danes. Her favourite was an Irish Wolfhound called Shadow.

Frederick II (1534–88)

King of Denmark and Norway. Frederick II of Denmark was greatly loved by his people and a good king but is probably best known internationally as the father of Anne of Denmark who became the queen of JAMES I of Great Britain and Ireland. He also caused considerable controversy when he created an order of chivalry in honour of his dog Wilpret.

Frederick II (1712–86)

King of Prussia. Frederick the Great, who came to the throne in 1740, was not only a powerful and fearless general (he had three horses killed under him in battle in 1758–9) but was also renowned for his court at Sans Souci Palace in Potsdam, near Berlin. On the ceiling at Sans Souci (which means 'free from care' – though German, Frederick only spoke French) is a painting of a spider, in honour of the spider that fell into his drinking chocolate which had been poisoned by his cook, thereby saving Frederick's life.

Frederick was also very fond of his female English greyhounds, one of which was called Alcmene. One of his favourite dogs was Biche, and imaginary letters were written by Frederick and his sister Wilhelmine, between Biche and her own dog, the spaniel Folichon. Biche was kidnapped during the Battle of Soor in 1745 by the Austrian General Radaski but was later recovered (she died in 1752). Frederick also wrote a poem to his greyhound Diane when she gave birth in 1769 and a fable, 'The Two Dogs and the Man' (1762).

Frederick was so fond of his dogs that from 1744 he had 11 white marble tombs erected in Sans Souci to their memory and his last wish was to be buried with them (and a favourite horse) at Sans Souci. However, this was denied him until 1991, 205 years after his death, when Germany was reunified. (His sister also erected a tomb to her dog Folichon at Bayreuth when it died in 1736.)

Frederick also kept a camel at Sans Souci.

George II (1683–1760)

King of Great Britain and Ireland. Known as the 'Little Captain', George II was the last British monarch to lead troops into battle, and when his horse bolted he led them on foot. A keen horseman and a good hunter, he also kept turkeys at Bushey Park. One of his sons, the Duke of Cumberland, once hunted a stag in Windsor Great Park with a tiger. When the tiger was wounded by the stag the Duke was so impressed that he had a silver collar engraved with details of this feat, put it on the stag and set it free. The Duke was also a successful breeder and set up a stud in Windsor Park which produced the famous colt Eclipse (named after the 1764 eclipse) but he died before the horse ran. Two of the three most important sires from which today's top thoroughbred horses are descended were Eclipse and Herod, both bred by the Duke.

George's mistress, the Countess of Suffolk, owned a dog called Marquise.

George III (1738–1820)

King of the United Kingdom. The first British monarch since Queen Anne to be born and educated in England, he was known as 'Farmer George' because of his interest in farming. George also enjoyed riding. The poet ALEXANDER POPE presented George's father Frederick, Prince of Wales, with one of the puppies of his Great Dane Bounce when Frederick was living in Kew Palace. The dog had a couplet by Pope inscribed on its collar:

> I am his Highness's dog at Kew.
> Pray tell me, sir, whose dog are you?

It was George III who was king when Britain lost her American colonies. The madness which affected him in later life took many forms including uttering the word 'peacock' at the end of each sentence, though it is not known what his views were on this particular bird. In 1767, when they were living in Kew, George's German wife, Queen Charlotte, imported two Pomeranian dogs, Phoebe and Mercury, into the country and these were painted a number of times by THOMAS GAINSBOROUGH, who lived nearby.

George IV (1762–1830)

King of the United Kingdom. The son of GEORGE III, George IV was keen on riding and horseracing – his horse won the Derby in 1788. However, he also suffered from delusions and claimed to have ridden a winner at Goodwood and even boasted to the DUKE OF WELLINGTON that he had led a battalion at Waterloo. George kept a large stables at his Brighton Pavilion home on the Sussex coast.

George V (1865–1936)

King of Great Britain. The son of EDWARD VII, George V was, like his father, a keen supporter of horseracing. Indeed, it was George V's horse, Anmer, under which Suffragette protester Emily Davidson threw herself (and was killed) at Tattenham Corner in Derby at Epsom, Surrey, on 4 June 1913. In 1928 his horse, Scuttle, won the Thousand Guineas race at Newmarket, and another (Limelight) won the Hardwicke Stakes at Ascot and other races. When he died his favourite white horse formed part of the funeral procession.

George owned a succession of dogs named Bob. He also bred clumber and springer spaniels at Sandringham and often entered them for dog shows. The most notable among these being Sandringham Stow, Sandringham Spark (a clumber which won first prize at Crufts in 1932 and 1934) and Sandringham Scion. The king named all his dogs himself and his Labradors won many prizes at Crufts – Wolferton Dan, Wolferton Ben and Wolferton Titus all became champions.

George VI (1895–1952)

King of Great Britain. When Duke of York in 1933 George bought the first of a long line of Pembroke Welsh corgis for which the current royal family are famed. A male originally called Rozavel Golden Eagle, he was later renamed Dookie, allegedly in retaliation by George's wife ELIZABETH (the late Queen Mother) against Wallis Simpson, the wife of George's older brother EDWARD VIII when Duke of Windsor after his abdication in 1936. Mrs Simpson's secret name for Elizabeth was apparently Cookie and the dog was supposedly named Dookie after the way Mrs Simpson (an American) pronounced Edward's title (Dukie). He was joined by Jane in 1938 and their puppies were Crackers and Carol. (In later years, when Crackers became old and infirm, Queen Elizabeth had a miniature Bath chair made for the dog so that it could be pushed around the garden.) George and Elizabeth also had a shih-tzu called Choo-Choo, so named because it made a noise like a train when breathing.

A keen dog-breeder, George's favourite Labradors at the Royal Lodge, Windsor, were Mipsy, Scrummy and Stiffy. Windsor Bob was the 1948 Kennel Club Field Champion. So devoted to his dogs was George that when one of his dogs injured its paw during a hare shoot on 5 February 1952 the king twice visited the kennels that frosty night to see if the dog was all right. The next morning the king died.

Henry II (1133–89)

King of England. The founder of the Plantagenet dynasty, who came to the throne in 1154, was a keen horseman and established the Royal Buckhounds, a pack which continued to hunt for the next eight centuries.

Henry III (1551–89)

King of France. The brother and successor of CHARLES IX and the last of the Valois line, Henry was assassinated by a fanatical priest. He had three favourite dogs – Liline, Titi and Mimi – which slept on his bed. Henry spent 100,000 écus a year on his birds and dogs and in 1586 owned 300 dogs. These were mostly miniature breeds and it is said that when he went out for his daily walk with Queen Louise he would take more than 20 of these with him in a specially made basket.

Henry IV (1553–1610)

King of France. The first Bourbon king of France, who was at various times a Huguenot (Protestant) or a Catholic, depending on the political situation – and was later assassinated by a religious fanatic – owned a pug dog called Soldat (French for 'soldier'). He also had a spaniel called Citron, who featured in a poem by Agrippa d'Aubigny (1552–1630), and another dog, Famor.

Henry VIII (1491–1547)

King of England, Wales and Ireland. The son of HENRY VII, 'Bluff King Hal', who was famously married six times, was particularly keen on hunting deer and stags and established his own pack of hounds, the Privy or Household Pack. Later in life when he was too fat to hunt from a horse he shot deer on foot, driven past by dogs. He even drained a marsh to form St James's Park and stocked it with deer. He was also keen on hawking and shooting birds. In addition he kept greyhounds both to race and as pets and owned a spaniel called Cutte and another dog called Ball. It is said that liver-and-white toy spaniels were first introduced to Britain by his fourth wife, Anne of Cleves, when they were married in 1540.

Henry is also supposed to have sent more than 400 dogs to the King of Spain to help with his war against France.

James I (1566–1625)

King of Great Britain and Ireland. The son of MARY QUEEN OF SCOTS, James came to the throne on the death of ELIZABETH I. He was a keen hunter and one of his favourite hounds appears in a picture of the time with James and his son, the future CHARLES I. Another, called Jowler, was kidnapped. However his special pet was yet another hound, Jewell, which died in 1613 when it was accidentally shot by his wife Anne of Denmark (daughter of FREDERICK II), when she was out hunting deer. He also owned an Arab horse called Markham. Queen Anne kept a number of dogs as pets and in a portrait of her by

Paul van Somer she is seen with five black-and-white miniature greyhounds which each have the letters 'AR' (for Anna Regina) embossed on their collars.

James II (1633–1701)

King of Great Britain and Ireland. The second son of CHARLES I, James was a keen hunter (he was one of the first British aristocrats to hunt foxes – until then stags had been the usual quarry) and enjoyed horseracing. One of his favourite pets was a springer spaniel dog called Mumper.

John (1199–1216)

King of England. Also known as John Lackland, he was a very unpopular king and it was during his reign that the barons forced him to sign the Magna Carta – the basis of the English constitution. King John was a keen horseman and also owned a pack of 240 greyhounds.

Louis XI (1423–83)

King of France. Louis unified France and founded three universities. He also owned a greyhound called Souillard which features in its own 'autobiography', one of the first ever written about a dog. Another greyhound called Mistodin had its own bed and bedclothes. When Louis died his favourite dog was buried with him – a sign of great respect by the owner, no doubt, but it is not recorded whether the dog felt the same way!

Louis XII (1462–1515)

King of France. Louis was married to Mary Tudor, the younger sister of HENRY VIII of England, but died soon after the wedding. Like LOUIS XI he also owned a greyhound (Relais) which 'wrote' its own autobiography.

Louis XIII (1601–43)

King of France. The father of LOUIS XIV, Louis's reign was dominated (from 1624) by the figure of his chief minister CARDINAL RICHELIEU. Louis was brought up in a household full of dogs – among those owned by his dominant mother, Marie de Medici, were Turquette, Negrite, Brigantin (which had its own stool next to her seat at the royal dinner table) and a greyhound called Bichette, which once gave birth to a puppy with two noses. As a seven-year-old boy Louis had his own miniature carriage pulled by two dogs, Pataut and Lion. Later he also had a miniature black greyhound called Charbon and other dogs included Cavalon, Soldat and Isabelle (Isabelle appears in the portrait of him as a child in 1606) and the spaniels Gayan and Cadet.

Louis XIV (1638–1715)

King of France. Known as 'The Sun King', Louis was the greatest monarch of his time and during his long reign (72 years, the longest in European history) France became the most powerful state in Europe. He was very fond of horses and owned a number of dogs including Pistolet, Silvie, Mignonne, Princesse and Dolinde.

Louis XIV's daughter-in-law, the Duchess of Maine, was a great cat-lover. When her favourite cat Marlemain died, the poet François de la Mothe le Vayer wrote its epitaph:

Puss passer-by, within this simple tomb
　　Lies one whose life fell Atropos hath shred;
The happiest cat on earth hath heard her doom,
　　And sleeps for ever in a marble bed.
Alas! what long delicious days I've seen!
　　O cats of Egypt, my illustrious sires,
You who on altars, bound with garlands green,
　　Have melted hearts, and kindled fond desires –
Hymns in your praise were paid, and offerings too,
　　But I'm not jealous of those rights divine,
Since Ludovisa loved me, close and true,
　　Your ancient glory was less proud than mine.
To live a simple pussy by her side
Was nobler far than to be deified.

Louis XV (1710–74)

King of France. Known as Louis the Well-Beloved, his reign witnessed the flourishing of the age of Rococo design (known as 'Louis XV style') and the loss of France's colonies in America and India. He owned at least three miniature greyhounds, Misse, Turlu and Zette – the last-named of which slept in a gilded bronze bed lined with crimson velvet. Another dog, a spaniel called Filou, had a gold collar studded with diamonds. Louis also had a cat called Collègue which he took to council meetings.

Louis's daughter, Princess Marie Adelaide, owned a papillon dog which appears in her portrait by Nattier (1740).

Louis's most famous mistress was another dog-lover, Madame de Pompadour (1721–64). Born Jeanne Antoinette Poisson she became a queen of fashion. After attracting the eye of the king at a ball she subsequently became his mistress with considerable influence on public affairs. A patroness of the arts who famously said 'Après nous le déluge!' she also saved the life of the playwright Prosper Jolyot de Crébillon (1674–1762) by giving him a pension when he was starving to death in an attic with 10 dogs, 15 cats and several ravens. Madame de Pompadour herself owned two female papillon dogs called Iñez (black and white) and Mimi (black and brown with a solid silver collar), both of which appear in portraits of her – and on their own in a painting by Jean-Jacques Bachelier (1759). She also kept a parrot and a monkey.

Louis XVI (1754–93)

King of France. Louis and his wife Marie-Antoinette (1755–93) were guillotined by revolutionaries led by MAXIMILIEN ROBESPIERRE in 1893. Among Marie-Antoinette's pet dogs were the pug Mops and a spaniel named Thisbée (named after the lover of Pyramus in the classic story in Ovid's *Metamorphoses*) which she kept in her bedroom and was a gift from the Princesse de Lamballe. She once famously remarked – in reply to the cry that the people were starving and had no bread – 'Let them eat cake'. It is not recorded what she fed her dogs on but they were all exceedingly well looked after and each had its own diamond-studded collar.

Ludwig II (1845–86)

King of Bavaria. 'Mad King Ludwig' was fond of animals but disliked dogs. As a child he had a pet tortoise. Like his whole family he was very fond of swans and named his fairytale castle Neuschwanstein (New Swan Castle) in their honour. He also owned peacocks and had a parrot that imitated his loud nervous laugh. He once invited his favourite grey mare, Cosa Rara, to dine with him on soup, fish and roast meat. A keen horseman he also owned a horse-drawn golden rococo sleigh decorated with cherubs which he would drive at night through the streets at great speed.

Mary Queen of Scots (1542–87)

Queen of Scotland. ELIZABETH I's great rival for the throne of England, and mother of JAMES I, when Mary was married to Francis II of France she owned 22 Maltese lapdogs and after her husband's death brought some with her to Scotland in 1561. Mary also kept spaniels, bloodhounds, turtle doves, Barbary fowls and caged birds. She fed her dogs on two loaves of bread a day (it was not usual then to feed dogs on meat). When Mary was executed at Fotheringhay Castle, Northamptonshire, one of her dogs crept out of the folds of her clothes and lay in the blood between her severed head and her body. As William Cecil, Lord Burghley, reported in his account of the event:

> Then one of the executioners, pulling off her garters, espied her little dogg, which was crept under her clothes, which could not be gotten forth but by force, yet afterwards would not depart from the corpse, but came and lay betweene her head and her shoulders, which being imbrued with her bloode was caryed away and washed, as all things ells were that had any bloode was either burned or clean washed.

She also had a palfrey called Black Agnes – given her by the Earl of Moray and named after Agnes of Dunbar – and another, her favourite, called Rosabelle.

Napoleon I (1769–1821)

French emperor. Napoleon's favourite mount was Marengo, a white Arabian stallion, which he rode at the beginning of the Battle of Waterloo even though the horse was then 22 years old. The horse was captured after the battle and taken to Britain and eventually died at the age of 29. Marengo's tiny skeleton (Napoleon was a very small man) can still be seen in the National Army Museum, London. Though Napoleon is depicted riding a white charger across the Alps in the famous painting by Vernet, this is complete propaganda as Napoleon actually crossed the pass on a mule. Napoleon also rode a white Arabian mare called Désirée.

Napoleon's first wife Josephine had a pug dog called Fortuné which bit the emperor in bed on their wedding night as it thought Bonaparte was attacking its mistress. Josephine later had a number of pugs which all slept in her bedroom on cashmere shawls and she also owned a monkey which had its own basket.

Napoleon also reputedly hated cats. The story goes that when staying in the palace of Schönbrunn after occupying Vienna following the Battle of Wagram, his cries of alarm late at night brought servants running to help only to discover him lunging with his sword at a cat which was hiding behind a tapestry on the wall.

When a child, Napoleon's son, the Duke of Rome, had a carriage pulled by sheep which were trained by Franconi, a famous circus trainer of the day.

Napoleon III (1808–73)

Emperor of the French. The third son of Louis Bonaparte, King of Holland (brother of NAPOLEON I), his wife the Empress Eugénie owned a Maltese dog called Linda which slept on her bed and is shown with her in a painting of the beach at Trouville by Eugene Boudin.

Nicholas I (1796–1855)

Tsar of Russia. Nicholas I, whose ambitions in Europe led to the Crimean War between Russia and the allied forces of Britain and France during the reign of QUEEN VICTORIA, owned a Russian Blue cat called Vashka.

Nicholas II (1868–1918)

Tsar of Russia. The last of the tsars of Russia and the grandson of QUEEN VICTORIA (and cousin of GEORGE V and Kaiser Wilhelm II), Nicholas and his family owned a number of dogs including a greyhound called Lofki and a spaniel called Joy which was a particular favourite of his haemophiliac son, Alex. Nicholas's wife Alexandra also had a borzoi called Minka which once bit the 'mad monk' Rasputin. They also had a cat called Kotka.

When the family were assassinated by Communists in 1918 a chin dog Jimmy – which one of the children had been holding – was also shot, but Joy survived and was later brought to England, where, blind, it lived out its days near Windsor. Nicholas also had a dog called Iman and a favourite horse was named Raven.

Peter I (1672–1725)

Tsar of Russia. Peter the Great's many achievements included the building of St Petersburg and making it the Russian capital after his mother's family had been murdered in the Kremlin, Moscow. For such a tall man (he stood six feet seven inches high) he owned a surprisingly small dog – a brown-coloured miniature Italian greyhound called Finette.

Philip V (1683–1746)

King of Spain. The first Bourbon (French) king of Spain, Philip was the grandson of LOUIS XIV. His second wife, Elizabeth Farnese of Parma, had a favourite lapdog called Liseta which had its portrait painted, lying on a crimson cushion, by Jean Ranc.

Rama V (1853–1910)

King of Siam. The royal family of Siam (modern Thailand) had long kept Siamese cats and in 1884 the first Siamese cats from the country's official royal cattery appeared in Britain. These were a parting gift from King Rama V (Somdeth Phra Paraminda Maha Chulalongkorn) to the then British Consul, Owen Gould. They were two sealpoints called Pho and Mia.

Richard II (1338–1410)

King of England. Richard, who succeeded his grandfather EDWARD III aged ten and was king of England as a teenager during the Peasants' Revolt, had a favourite greyhound called Mathe. His favourite horse was called Roan Barbary and is mentioned in Shakespeare's *Richard II*:

When Bolingbroke rode on Roan Barbary,
That horse that thou so often hast bestrid.

Richard III (1452–85)

King of England. The brother of Edward IV, and reputedly responsible for the murder of Edward's son Edward V and his brother, Richard met his end at Bosworth Field, Leicestershire, in 1485 – the last English king to die in battle – where his opponent was Henry Tudor (later Henry VII), father of HENRY VIII. It was Richard who famously said in Shakespeare's play about him: 'A horse! a horse! my kingdom for a horse!' after he had lost his favourite mount White Surrey in the battle. In *Richard III* (Act V, Scene 3) this stallion is mentioned: 'Saddle White Surrey for the field to-morrow.' Richard's emblem was a white boar which led to the famous couplet:

The catte, the ratte, and Lovell our dogge
Rulyth all Englande under a hogge.

(The cat was William Catesby, the rat was Sir Richard Ratcliffe, while Francis Viscount Lovell was known as 'the King's spaniel'. All were advisors to the king.)

Prince Rupert (1619–82)

Royalist general. The nephew of CHARLES I and grandson of JAMES I, Prince Rupert of the Rhine fought on the Royalist side during the English Civil War. He had a large white poodle called Boy which is held to be the first poodle ever seen in England. Boy was given to the Prince by Lord Arundel (English ambassador in Vienna) when Rupert was imprisoned in Linz, Austria, for three years. He became his constant companion in jail and on his release in 1642 came to England with his master when Rupert was summoned to help his uncle during the Civil War. Believed to have magical powers, Boy was later killed at the Battle of Marston Moor on 2 July 1644 and his death is commemorated in a Puritan poem 'A Dog's Elegy or Rupert's Tears' (1644).

Rupert also had two greyhounds which went missing in 1667 and whose loss was announced in the *London Gazette* with a reward offered for their safe return. They were described as being 'the one a large white young Dog, with a thick black head, with a chain and small coller: the other a cole black Dog with a small coller'.

Prince Dhuleep Singh (1838–93)

Maharajah of Lahore. Prince Dhuleep Singh was the last emperor of the Sikhs, who gave QUEEN VICTORIA the most famous diamond in the world – the Koh-i-Noor (Persian for 'mountain of light') – now kept in the Tower of London. Singh owned a poodle called Froggy.

Queen Victoria (1819–1901)

Queen of Great Britain. As a child Victoria had a dog called Fanny. As a 13-year-old girl, she became very fond of a tricolour Cavalier King Charles spaniel called Dash which had been given to her mother, the Duchess of Kent, in 1833. In 1836 her mother commissioned SIR EDWIN LANDSEER to paint the dog's portrait for Victoria's 17th birthday. Victoria became Queen in 1837. The first thing she did after her coronation in Westminster Abbey the following year was to rush back to Buckingham Palace to give the dog a bath. Sometimes she dressed Dash in blue trousers and a red jacket. When the dog died in 1840 it was buried in Windsor Park under a marble effigy with an inscription which ended:

READER
If you would be beloved and regretted
Profit by the example of
DASH

In 1839 Landseer painted a picture entitled 'Queen Victoria's Favourite Pets' which featured Dash seated on a footstool together with a parrot (Lory), a deerhound and Eos, the favourite female greyhound of Prince Albert. Eos also appears in Landseer's childhood portrait of the queen's daughter, Princess Victoria (1841). Dark brown with a white neck and white feet, when the dog died in 1844 a monument by the sculptor John Francis was erected to its memory at Windsor.

Victoria also had a fawn-and-white female Pekinese, the first to be seen in the West, called Lootie. Given to her

in 1861 after the dog had been discovered when the Summer Palace in Peking had been ransacked, the queen also commissioned a portrait of her. In addition she had a number of Skye terriers, the first being Scotty and others were called Cairnach, Islay, Boz and, her favourite, Dandie Dinmont (after the character who bred terriers in the popular novel *Guy Mannering* by SIR WALTER SCOTT). Her favourite collie was Sharp whose portrait was exhibited at the Royal Academy. Greyhounds owned by Victoria included Nero and Hector. She also bred deerhounds and entered two of these into the first-ever dog show in New York in 1877.

In addition Victoria had a Chinese pug called King Dick which was an extremely efficient rat-catcher (during her long reign she owned no less than 36 pugs), a dachshund called Däckel which died in 1859 aged 15, and in 1893 had a fox-terrier called Spot, a collie named Roy and a toy poodle, Marco. At various times she also owned a German Boar-hound (Vulcan), a Newfoundland (Nelson), a bloodhound (Hotspur), a St Bernard (Maurice), a number of dachshunds (including

Dacko and Waldman), two white collies (Snowball and Nanny), a border collie (Fern), a Pomeranian (Janey), a fox-terrier (Wat) and a Maltese dog called Chico. A Pyrenean Mountain Dog called Gabbas (a gift from King Louis-Philippe of France in 1844) did little to cement Anglo-French relations as no sooner had it arrived than it bit Victoria's arm and was subsequently given to the Zoological Society.

Other dogs in the royal household were clumber spaniels which Prince Albert first introduced to the royal shoots at Windsor and Balmoral. A life-size marble sculpture of a large dog called Noble (one of a number of border collies of that name) stands in Victoria's former home, Osborne House, on the Isle of Wight. So realistic is the sculpture that the staff are constantly having to clean it after visitors stroke the stone dog.

In 1897 the Royal Stables at Buckingham Palace contained 120 horses including Zulu and Kassassin (black males) and the creams Occo (the largest), King George, Emperor, Amarongen, Monarch, Majestic, Sovereign and Middachten. The rest were all bays including Blytheswood and Bullion. By contrast the stables at Windsor – about 40 horses – contained mostly greys. Victoria also had a 'garden-chair' at Windsor pulled by a black Exmoor pony about 12 hands high called Sam. Other pet ponies were the mare Fidget and the 30-year-old Jessie, whom the queen had been very fond of riding. An especial favourite of the royal children was the Maltese donkey Prince, who used to take them for rides in a miniature barouche. The queen's favourite official mount was a white horse called Leopold.

One of the most fervent supporters of the National Cat Club Victoria also possessed two Persian cats, Flypie and White Heather, which were inherited by her son, EDWARD VII, on her death in 1901. However, at the end of her life it was her dogs that gave her most comfort and she asked for her favourite Pomeranian, Turi, to be brought to her in her final hours.

Victoria's daughter, Princess Louise (1848–1939), who married John Campbell, Duke of Argyll, owned a collie dog.

William the Conqueror (c. 1027–87)

King of England. William had an 'inordinate appetite for the Chase' and was especially fond of deer-hunting. A keen horseman, he had three horses killed under him at the Battle of Hastings in 1066 and eventually died after injuries sustained when he was thrown against the pommel of his horse's saddle in Rouen, France, in August 1087. His son William II (William Rufus) also died on his horse, after being shot by an arrow in a supposed riding accident while hunting in the New Forest in 1100 (in reality he was probably assassinated).

William III (1650–1702)

King of England. The Protestant William of Orange was the son of CHARLES I's oldest daughter Mary and ruled England with his wife Mary (daughter of JAMES II and sister of QUEEN ANNE) after James had been deposed. When he landed in Torbay in 1688 he brought with him a number of pug dogs. A keen hunter who once imported 108 deer to add to the stock at Windsor Park, William died after breaking his collarbone in a fall when his favourite horse, the one-eyed Sorrel, stumbled on a molehill in the park at Hampton Court. In the reign of his successor Queen Anne a favourite Jacobite toast was to the 'Little Gentleman in Velvet' who had made the molehill that led to William's death (the Jacobites were supporters of the Catholic James II). William also owned racehorses, and among his winners were Turk and the unlikely named Stiff Dick.

Queen Mary also owned a dog called True, which had its epitaph written by Matthew Prior (1664–1721), one of the first poems to be written in praise of a pet.

Poets

Matthew Arnold (1822–88)

British poet and critic. Son of the famous teacher Thomas Arnold, whose period as headmaster of Rugby School is evoked in Thomas Hughes' novel *Tom Brown's Schooldays*, Matthew Arnold is best known as the author of such poems as 'Dover Beach'. He also owned a number of pets including a canary called Matthias and a Persian cat called Atossa or Toss (named after the daughter of Cyrus the Great who became the wife of Darius). He even wrote a poem about the two animals, 'Poor Matthias' (1882) – including a reference to another pet, a brown dog called Rover. In it he describes how Atossa would sit beside the bird's cage:

> Poor Matthias! Wouldst thou have
> More than pity? claim'st a stave?
> – Friends more near us than a bird
> We dismiss'd without a word.
> Rover, with the good brown head,
> Great Atossa, they are dead;
> Dead, and neither prose nor rhyme
> Tells the praises of their prime.
> Thou didst know them old and grey,
> Know them in their sad decay.
> Thou hast seen Atossa sage
> Sit for hours beside thy cage;
> Thou wouldst chirp, thou foolish bird,
> Flutter, chirp – she never stirr'd!
> What were now these toys to her?
> Down she sank amid her fur;
> Eyed thee with a soul resigned –

And thou deemedst cats were kind!
– Cruel, but composed and bland,
Dumb, inscrutable and grand,
So Tiberius might have sat,
Had Tiberius been a cat.

Arnold also had a brown-and-black dachshund called Geist who appears in the same poem but in addition features in 'Geist's Grave' (1881). Two other dachshunds in his house in Cobham were Max and the black-and-brown Kaiser:

Max a dachshund without blot –
Kaiser should be, but is not.
Max, with shining yellow coat,
Prinking ears and dewlap throat –
Kaiser, with his collie face,
Penitent for want of race.

Kaiser (who died in 1887) also appears in 'Kaiser Dead', Arnold's last poem and written the year before his own death. He also owned cats and said of one:

If I let her in and go on writing without taking notice of her, there is a real demonstration of affection for five minutes. She purrs, she walks round and round me, she jumps on my lap, she rubs her head and nose against my chin ...

However, Arnold's pets were not universally liked. The novelist Mrs Humphrey Ward, a niece of Arnold, described visits to his pretty cottage in Cobham:

The only drawback to the Cobham visits were the 'dear, dear boys'! – i.e. the dachshunds, Max and Geist, who, however adorable in themselves, had no taste for visitors and no intention of letting such intruding creatures interfere with their possession of their master. One would go down to Cobham, eager to talk to 'Uncle Matt' about a book or an article – covetous at any rate of *some* talk with him undisturbed. And it would all end in a breathless chase after Max, through field after field where the little wretch was harrying either sheep or cows, with the dear poet, hoarse with shouting, at his heels. The dogs were always *in the party*, talked to, caressed, or scolded exactly like spoilt children; and the cat of the house was almost equally dear.

W.H. Auden (1907–73)

British poet. Auden achieved fame in the 1930s, both as a solo poet and in collaboration with Christopher Isherwood on three plays, *The Dog Beneath the Skin*, *The Ascent of F6* and *On the Frontier*. He had a dog called Mosé and two cats, Rudimace and Leonora, named after characters in opera. Of Rudimace he once said: 'Cats can be very funny, and have the oddest ways of showing they're glad to see you. Rudimace always peed in our shoes.'

Charles Baudelaire (1821–67)

French poet and critic. A great lover of cats, Baudelaire also kept a pet bat in a cage on his desk. Three poems in his famous collection *Les Fleurs du Mal* (1857) are about cats and apparently every time he visited someone's house he would first of all greet the family cat. He also said 'It is easy to understand why the rabble dislike cats. A cat is beautiful, it suggests ideas of luxury, cleanliness, voluptuous pleasures.'

Rupert Brooke (1887–1915)

British poet. Best known for his poem 'The Soldier' ('If I should die, think only this of me ...') Brooke appears in a family photo of *c.* 1901 with two small, largely white terriers. His father William Parker Brooke was an eccentric schoolmaster at Rugby School who often took the family dog into his classes.

Elizabeth Barrett Browning (1806–61)

British poet. As a child Elizabeth Barrett kept a black pony called Moses. However, she fell when trying to saddle it on her own aged 15 and the resulting injury to her spine rendered her a semi-invalid thereafter.

Her most famous pet – and inseparable companion for 12 years – was her red male cocker spaniel Flush, a gift from the writer Mary Russell Mitford in about 1842, which was later the subject of a spoof autobiography *Flush* (1933), by Virginia Woolf. It also featured in two poems by Browning herself ('Flush, or Faunus' [1855] and 'To Flush, my dog' [1855]) where it is described as 'darkly brown' with hazel eyes. Flush bit Robert Browning twice while he was courting his mistress and was kidnapped three times. When the Brownings moved to Italy they took the dog with them but he did not like the countryside: 'Flush hated Vallombrosa, and was frightened out of his wits by the pine forests. Flush likes civilised life and the society of little dogs with turned up tails, such as Florence abounds with.' And in a letter from 1848 she describes his delight in the city:

He runs out in the piazza whenever he pleases and plays with the dogs when they are pretty enough, and wags his tail at the sentinels and civic guard, and takes the Grand Duke as a sort of neighbour of his, whom it is proper enough to patronise, but who has considerably less inherent merit and dignity than the spotted spaniel in the alley to the left.

Flush died in 1854 and was buried in a cellar beneath the Brownings' home in Florence, the Casa Guidi.

Robert Burns (1759–96)
Scottish poet. The author of 'Tam o' Shanter' and 'Auld Lang Syne' owned a pet ewe, called Poor Mailie, and her two lambs, which he bought from a neighbour when living in Lochlie. One day the sheep died after getting caught up in some wire and Burns wrote two poems

about her 'The Death and Dying Words of Poor Mailie' and 'Poor Mailie's Elegy'. He also had a male dog called Luath. A 'plough man's collie' named after Cuchillin's dog in the Fingal epic of 'Ossian' (James Macpherson), Luath was killed by a stranger's wanton cruelty on 12 February 1784. Burns included him in the poem 'The Twa Dogs' (1785) – though the other dog, Caesar, is entirely imaginary – and describes him thus:

> His breast was white, his towzie back,
> Weel clad wi' coat of glossy black.

Luath (whose name in Gaelic means 'swift' or 'nimble') tripped up Jean Armour at a wedding and gave Burns the chance to speak to the woman who was to become his wife and great love.

Lord Byron (1788–1824)

British poet. Author of such classics as *Don Juan* and *Childe Harold's Pilgrimage*, the great Romatic poet's best-known pet was his black-and-white Newfoundland dog Boatswain. He was always attacking Byron's mother's fox-terrier Gilpin until, fearing for his life, she sent the smaller dog away to live with a tenant. However, Boatswain then disappeared and returned with Gilpin, after which the two became great friends.

As a student at Trinity College, Cambridge, Byron had to leave Boatswain behind as dogs were not allowed – he kept a bear instead. He wrote about his new pet to Elizabeth Pigot on 26 October 1807: 'I have got a new

friend, the finest in the world, a tame bear. When I brought him here they asked me what I meant to do with him and my reply was, "He should sit for a fellowship".' Byron used to walk him about Trinity College on a chain and later, when he moved into Newstead Abbey in September 1808, installed a plunge bath in which he often played with the bear.

Boatswain eventually died after suffering a fit in 1808 and Byron had him buried in a tomb intended for himself at the family seat at Newstead Abbey, Nottinghamshire. He even composed an epitaph for him which read:

Near this spot
Are deposited the remains of one
Who possessed Beauty without vanity,
Strength without insolence,
Courage without ferocity,
And all the virtues of Man without his Vices.
This praise, which would be unmeaning Flattery

If inscribed over human ashes,

Is but a just tribute to the memory of

Boatswain, a Dog,

Who was born at Newfoundland, May 1803

And died at Newstead Abbey, 18 Nov, 1808.

When living in Ravenna, Italy (where he was visited by Shelley in 1821) he had five peacocks, two guinea fowl, three monkeys, eight dogs, five cats, a crow, a falcon and an Egyptian crane in the house. When he went to Greece to fight in the War of Independence he took with him a Newfoundland called Lyon and a bulldog called Moretto. He also owned a mongrel sheepdog called Mutz, ten horses, an eagle, a parrot, a goat, a badger and three geese.

Samuel Taylor Coleridge (1772–1834)

British poet and philosopher. The author of 'Kublai Khan', and 'The Rime of the Ancient Mariner' among other classic poems, there is no record of what pets, if any, the great Romantic poet kept. However, he was a great friend of ROBERT SOUTHEY (they married two sisters) who was a well-known cat-lover, and WILLIAM WORDSWORTH who also kept animals and with whom Coleridge lived for some time. His son Hartley Coleridge (1796–1849), who was also a poet, had a cat called Nellie and wrote a poem about it 'To a Cat' which begins:

Nellie, methinks, 'twixt thee and me

There is a kind of sympathy;

And could we interchange our nature –

If I were a cat, thou human creature –
I should, like thee, be no great mouser,
And thou, like me, no great composer ...

William Cowper (1731–1800)

British poet. Probably best known for his poems 'John Gilpin' and 'The Olney Hymns', Cowper had a spaniel called Beau who featured in a number of his verses such as 'The Dog and the Water Lily' and 'On a Spaniel Called Beau Killing a Young Bird'. The former poem was based on a real incident when Cowper had tried and failed to get some waterlilies from a river. He wrote about it in a letter of 1787:

> Returning soon after toward the same place, I observed him plunge into the river, while I was about forty yards distant from him; and when I had reached the spot, he swam to land with a lily in his mouth, which he came and laid at my foot.

At the end of his life Cowper also owned three male leverets which were given him by neighbours after recovering from a period of mental illness. Called Puss, Tiney and Bess, he described them in an article in the *Gentleman's Magazine* in June 1784:

> I always admitted them into the parlour after supper, when, the carpet affording their feet a firm hold, they would frisk, and bound, and play a thousand gambols, in which Bess, being remarkably strong and fearless, was always superior to the rest, and proved himself the Vestris of the party. One

evening the cat, being in the room, had the hardiness to pat Bess upon the cheek, an indignity which he resented by drumming upon her back with such violence, that the cat was happy to escape from under his paws, and hide herself.

Tiney was immortalised in his poem 'Epitaph on a Hare' when it died aged nine.

Cowper was also fond of cats and wrote at least two poems on them: 'The Colubriad' – featuring three kittens – and 'The Retired Cat'. The latter poem begins:

A poet's cat, sedate and grave,
As poet well could wish to have,
Was much addicted to inquire
For nooks, to which she might retire,
And where, secure as mouse in chink,
She might repose, or sit and think.
I know not where she caught the trick –
Nature perhaps herself had cast her
In such a mould *philosophique*,
Or else she learn'd it of her master.
Sometimes ascending, debonair,
An apple-tree or lofty pear.
Lodg'd with convenience in the fork,
She watched the gard'ner at his work;
Sometimes her ease and solace sought
In an old empty wat'ring pot,
There wanting nothing save a fan,
To seem some nymph in her sedan,
Aparell'd in exactest sort
And ready to be borne to court.

W.H. Davies (1871–1940)

British-born poet. The one-legged author of *Auto-biography of a Supertramp* (1908) and other works owned a cat called Venus and also wrote a number of poems about cats. He also wrote about dogs.

Emily Dickinson (1830–86)

This reclusive New England poet (only 7 of her 2000 poems were published in her lifetime) had a dog called Carlo who died in 1866. One of her best known poems about a cat is 'She Sights a Bird':

> She sights a Bird – she chuckles –
> She flattens – then she crawls –
> She runs without the look of feet –
> Her eyes increase to Balls –
>
> Her Jaws stir – twitching – hungry –
> Her Teeth can hardly stand –
> She leaps, but Robin leaped the first –
> Ah, Pussy, of the Sand,
>
> The Hopes so juicy ripening –
> You almost bathed your Tongue –
> When Bliss disclosed a hundred Toes –
> And fled with every one –

John Drinkwater (1882–1937)

British poet and critic. John Drinkwater had a cat called Punch. When he was ill in bed one day, his friend EDMUND GOSSE wrote to him:

> I hope you will take the greatest possible care of yourself, and obey Dr Punch, whose expressed view I know to be that you should stay in bed and make warm corners in the coverlid for him to fold his paws into.

Joachim du Bellay (1522–60)

French poet. Du Bellay was one the famous Pleiades group of writers in France and wrote their manifesto, defending the use of French as a suitable language for literary expression. He wrote the first-ever sonnet sequence in French (*L'Olive*, 1549–50) and by coincidence was also the first person to write poetry in praise of a cat, the pet in question being his silver-grey tom called Belaud. When the cat died he wrote a 200-verse poem in its memory. Here is an extract:

> Three days ago I lost
> All that I value most.
> My treasure, my delight;
> I cannot speak or write,
> Or even think of what
> Belaud, my small grey cat
> Meant to me, tiny creature.
> Masterpiece of nature
> In the whole world of cats –
> And certain death to rats! –
> Whose beauty was worthy
> Of immortality.

T.S. Eliot (1888–1965)

US-born poet. The author of *The Waste Land* (1922), *Four Quartets* (1944) and *Old Possum's Book of Practical Cats* (1939) – which gave rise to Andrew Lloyd Webber's 1981 musical *Cats* – himself owned many cats. Among these were Wiscus, Pettipaws and George

Pushdragon (a pseudonym Eliot used when entering crossword competitions). When living at 57 Chester Terrace, Belgravia, the Eliots had two Yorkshire terriers, Peter and Polly Louise, and a cat called George.

Roy Fuller (1912–91)

British poet. Roy Fuller, whose work was influenced by W.H. AUDEN and Stephen Spender, and who was professor of Poetry at Oxford University from 1968 to 1973, had a cat called Domino which is remembered in his poem 'In Memory of My Cat Domino: 1951-66'.

Théophile Gautier (1811–72)

French poet, novelist and critic. Gautier's most famous collection of poems was *Emaux et camées* (1852, *Enamels and Cameos*) and he was also well known for his novel *Mademoiselle de Maupin* (1835). A great cat-lover he owned nine cats including the white Don Pierrot, the silver-grey Zizi, Enjolras, Gavroche and the black-haired Eponine, the last three named after characters in *Les Misérables* by VICTOR HUGO. Another female was the snow-white Séraphita (named after the heroine of the romance by HONORÉ DE BALZAC) whom he describes in *La Ménagerie Intime* as being 'of a dreamy disposition ... delighted in perfumes ... walked upon the dressing-table among the scent bottles, smelling the stoppers'. Childebrand was 'a splendid gutter-cat, short-haired, striped black and tan ... His great green eyes, with the almond-shaped pupils, and his regular velvet stripes, gave him a distant, tigerish look that I liked. "Cats are the tigers of poor fellows," I once wrote ...' However, his favourite was Madame Théophile, 'a reddish cat with a white breast, a pink nose and blue eyes, so called because she lived with us in an intimacy which was quite conjugal'. She also loved perfumes, especially patchouli and vetiver, but hated it when singers hit high notes. She would sit at the piano while they accompanied themselves but when they hit the high note A she would put her paw over their mouths.

Gautier once said, 'The cat is a dilettante in fur.' He also reputedly kept white rats.

Oliver Goldsmith (1728–74)

Irish-born poet, playwright and novelist. Goldsmith is best known for his novel *The Vicar of Wakefield* (1766), the poem 'The Deserted Village' (1770) and the play *She Stoops to Conquer* (1773). As a young man Goldsmith, who came from a very poor family, rode his horse from his home in Ballymahon 120 miles to Cork, intending to emigrate to the USA and make his fortune. However, after he had sold the horse to pay his passage, the ship was delayed in harbour waiting for favourable winds. Unfortunately the winds changed while Goldsmith was on a trip outside the city and he missed the boat. As a result he had to spend his last penny on a broken-down pony he called Fiddleback and return to his home. He also had a cat when studying medicine at Edinburgh University.

Gerard Manley Hopkins (1844–89)

British poet. Though none of his poems was published in his lifetime, some of the best-known works by Hopkins include 'The Wreck of the *Deutschland* and 'The Windhover'. Hopkins had a kitten that he rescued from his windowsill. As he recorded in his diary:

> Rescued a little kitten that was perched in the sill of the round window at the sink over the gasjet and dared not jump down. I heard her mew a piteous long time till I could bear it no longer; but I make a note of it because of her gratitude after I had taken her down, which made her follow me about and at each turn of the stairs as I went down leading her to the kitchen ran back a few steps up and try to get up to lick me through the banisters from the flight above.

John Keats (1795–1821)

British poet. That Keats was fond of animals is shown by such poems as 'Ode to a Nightingale'. His father also kept a livery stables and so he was brought up among horses. Keats was very fond of cats (the coat of arms of the Keats family was 'three wild cats passant in pale sable') but did not own one himself. However, when living in Hampstead with his friend Charles Brown a neighbour's cat was a frequent visitor to his room. The tabby also had a daughter which was black-and-white but only the mother ever visited Keats. As he remarked in a letter to his brother George in 1819:

Now it appears ominous to me for the doors of both houses are opened frequently – so that there is a complete thoroughfare for both cats (there being no board up to the contrary) they may one and several of them come into my room ad libitum. But no – the Tabby only comes – whether from sympathy from Ann the maid or me I can not tell ... I have questioned her – I have look'd at the lines of her paw – I have felt her pulse – to no purpose – why should the old cat come to me? I ask myself – and myself has not a word to answer.

Keats also wrote a poem 'On Mrs Reynolds' Cat' which begins:

Cat! who hast pass'd thy grand climacteric,
        How many mice and rats hast in thy days
        Destroy'd? – How many tit bits stolen? Gaze
With those bright languid segments green, and prick
Those velvet ears – but pr'ythee do not do stick
        Thy latent talons in me – and upraise
        Thy gentle mew – and tell me all thy frays
Of fish and mice, and rats and tender chick.
Nay, look not down, nor lick thy dainty wrists –
        For all the wheezy asthma, and for all
Thy tail's tip is nick'd off – and though the fists
        Of many a maid have given thee many a maul,
Still is that fur as soft as when the lists
        In youth thou enter'dst on glass bottled wall.

Walter Savage Landor (1775–1864)

British poet. Best-known for his prose dialogue *Imaginary Conversations* (1824–9), Landor had a number of dogs including an Alsatian. However, he preferred Pomeranians. His favourite was a small white male called Pomero which had been sent to him from his villa in Fiesola and with which he would talk in Italian and English when he lived in Bath. The dog used to watch people going to church and when Landor was away from home in 1844 he wrote to his friend John Forster:

> Daily do I think of Bath and Pomero. I fancy him lying on the narrow window-sill, and watching the good people go to church. He has not yet made up his mind between the Anglican and the Roman Catholic; but I hope he will continue in the faith of his forefathers, if it will make him happier.

Pomero lived for 12 years. When he died in 1856 Landor was deeply upset and the family cat lay night and day upon its grave. Landor wrote a Latin epitaph for Pomero and also wrote a poem for his successor, another Pomeranian called Giallo, who was his last dog. Landor also wrote: 'Next to servants, horses are the greatest trouble in life. Dogs are blessings, true blessings.'

When a young man, Landor had owned a striped tom called Cincirillo who killed the family's pet white pigeons, and features in a poem 'To My Child Carlino', addressed to his son:

> Carlino! What art thou about, my boy? ...
> Does Cincirillo follow thee about?

Inverting one swart foot suspensively,
And wagging his dread jaw, at every chirp
Of bird above him in the olive-branch?
Frighten him then away! 'twas he who slew
Our pigeons, our white pigeons, peacock-tailed,
That fear'd not you and me ... alas, nor him!
I flattened his striped sides along my knee,
And reasoned with him on his bloody mind,
Till he looked blandly, and half-closed his eyes
To ponder on my lecture in the shade.
I doubt his memory much, his heart a little
And in some minor matters (may I say it?)
Could wish him rather sager. But from thee
God hold back wisdom yet for many years!

Andrew Lang (1844–1912)

British poet and novelist. The author of the *Blue Fairy Book* (1889) and other works had 'a nefarious old cat' called Gyp and another called Mr Toby. He also had a dog called Dan.

Amy Lowell (1874–1925)

US poet. A free-verse poet who invented the phrase 'polyphonic prose', Lowell's works include *Sword Blades and Poppy Seed* (1914). She had a black cat with green eyes called Winky who features in her poem 'To Winky' in her book *Pictures of the Floating World* (1919), which begins:

You walk as a king scorning his subjects;

You flirt with me as a concubine in robes of silk.

Cat,

I am afraid of your poisonous beauty.

Stéphane Mallarmé (1842–98)

French poet. One of the leaders of the Symbolist school of poetry, Mallarmé's *L'Après-midi d'un faune* inspired CLAUDE DEBUSSY's prelude. He had a black cat called Lilith who was sketched by J.M. WHISTLER.

Comte Robert de Montesquiou-Fezensac (1855–1921)

French poet and critic. This aesthete and dandy, who was a former lover of SARAH BERNHARDT, kept a gilt tortoise which he would carry around with him. Painted by J.M. WHISTLER, Montesquiou was also the model for Baron de Charlus in *A là Recherche du Temps Perdu* by Proust and the Duc Jean Floressas des Esseintes in *A Rebours* by J.K. HUYSMANS.

Gérard de Nerval (1808–55)

French poet. De Nerval had a pet lobster which he would take for walks. He was once caught in the Palais-Royal in Paris with the lobster on a lead made from blue ribbon. When the gendarmes asked him why he had a lobster instead of a dog he replied:

Why should a lobster be any more ridiculous than a dog ... or any other animal that one chooses to take for a walk? I have a liking for lobsters. They are peaceful, serious creatures. They know the secrets of the sea, they don't bark, and they don't gnaw upon one's monadic privacy like dogs do. And Goethe had an aversion to dogs, and he wasn't mad.

However, de Nerval was more than a little unbalanced. He finally took his own life when he hanged himself from an apron string he thought was the Queen of Sheba's garter and they found his pet raven flying around his body crying the only words he had taught it: 'J'ai soif' ('I'm thirsty').

Petrarch (1304–74)

Italian poet. Famed for his love poems to Laura (an ancestor of the Marquis de Sade) Petrarch was also very fond of his pet cat, Arqua, and it was his only comfort when Laura died. Arqua was killed and mummified after Petrarch's death and set in a niche in his study. Beneath it a marble slab was inscribed 'Second only to Laura'. The Latin poet Antonious Quaeringus wrote a poem to the cat, part of which reads as follows:

> Through all my exemplary life,
> So well did I in constant strife
> > Employ my claws and curses,
> That even now though I am dead,
> Those nibbling wretches dare not tread,
> > On one of Petrarch's verses.

Alexander Pope (1688–1744)

British poet. Pope owned a succession of Great Danes called Bounce. He had bought the original dog after he had received threats following publication of his satirical poem *The Dunciad* (1728) in which he attacked other poets. When out walking near his house in Twickenham, the tiny, frail and crippled Pope would take the huge dog with him together with two pistols for protection. The dog features in his poem 'Bounce to Fop. An Heroick Epistle from a Dog at Twickenham to a Dog at Court' (*c.* 1736), the first poem ever written by a major British author to his own dog (Fop was a spaniel owned by Pope's friend Lady Suffolk). The second verse of this poem begins:

> Fop! you can dance, and make a Leg,
> Can fetch and carry, cringe and beg,
> And (what's the Top of all your Tricks)
> Can stoop to pick up Strings and Sticks.
> We country dogs love nobler sport,
> And scorn the Pranks of Dogs at Court ...

One of Bounce's puppies was presented to Frederick, Prince of Wales (father of GEORGE III), then living in nearby Kew Palace, with a couplet by Pope inscribed on its collar:

> I am his Highness's dog at Kew.
> Pray tell me, sir, whose dog are you?

When Pope was dying Bounce was looked after by his friend Lord Orrery. When the dog itself died Pope wrote the following verse to his kind keeper:

> Ah Bounce! ah gentle Beast! why wouldst thou dye,
> When thou had'st Meat enough and Orrery?

John Wilmot, 2nd Earl of Rochester
(1648–80)
British poet. Rochester wrote numerous songs, satires and poems and was a prominent member of the court of his day. He kept a monkey which appeared in a portrait of him by Jacob Huysmans.

Christina Rossetti (1830–94)
British poet. Christina Rossetti was the sister of the Pre-Raphaelite painter and poet Dante Gabriel Rossetti and a major poet in her own right with works such as *Goblin Market and Other Poems* and the famous carol 'In the Bleak Midwinter'. She also had a cat called Grimalkin which died while giving birth and whose passing was noted in her poem: 'On the Death of a Cat: A Friend of Mine Aged Ten Years and a Half' which contains the lines:

> Of a noble race she came,
> And Grimalkin was her name.
> Young and old full many a mouse
> Felt the prowess of her house;
> Weak and strong full many a rat

Cowered beneath her crushing pat;
And the birds around the place
Shrank from her too-close embrace.
But one night, reft of her strength,
She lay down and died at length:
Lay a kitten by her side
In whose life the mother died.

Dante Gabriel Rossetti (1828–82)

British poet and painter. One of the founders of the Pre-Raphaelite Brotherhood and brother of CHRISTINA ROSSETTI, Rossetti's father had once had a cat which had a peculiar habit. After returning from King's College London, each day – where he was Professor of Italian – Rossetti senior would collapse in his chair in front of the fire, whereupon the family cat would stretch out her forelegs in the shape of a capital Y, hook the claws of her front paws into the fireguard, and remain in this position until disturbed.

D.G. Rossetti was also a great animal lover and kept a vast menagerie of animals including an opossum that slept on the dining-room table, a racoon that lived in a drawer in a dresser, an armadillo, a peacock, a wombat, woodchucks, owls, a raven, a zebra, a donkey and a monkey – some of which lived in his house in Chelsea. He once announced that he wanted to buy an elephant so that he could teach it to wash the windows of the house. He also had a black-and-white cat called Zoe and – while living at Kelmscott Manor near Lechlade, Oxfordshire – kept three dogs (including Dizzy, a black-and-tan terrier).

Vita Sackville-West (1892–1962)

British poet and novelist. Best known for her novels *The Edwardians* (1930) and *All Passion Spent* (1931) and the poem 'The Land' (1926), Vita Sackville-West was the inspiration for her close friend VIRGINIA WOOLF's book *Orlando* (1928). She had a number of dogs and cats. In a letter to Virginia Woolf written in 1925 she describes how one day the five kittens of one of her cats and the seven puppies of her spaniel dog ended up in the same basket. Seeing that the cat had left her litter unattended, the dog carefully carried them in her mouth and deposited them with the puppies in her basket where she suckled them all together. However, when the dog went for a walk the cat reappeared, curled herself up in the dog's basket and suckled the puppies and the kittens herself. Then when the spaniel returned she chased out the cat and suckled the kittens and puppies again. As Sackville-West admitted to her friend, 'I find myself quite unable to cope with this situation.'

At the end of her life she also had an Alsatian called Martha (who was buried in the wood at her home, Sissinghurst in Kent, when she died), another called Rocco and a Saluki which was given to her by GERTRUDE STEIN in Baghdad. Her last book was *Faces: Profiles of Dogs* (1961).

Carl Sandburg (1878–1967)

US poet. Though a distinguished poet, Sandburg is probably best known for his six-volume biography of ABRAHAM LINCOLN. He also kept goats and was so fond of them that one night when it was freezing outside his home in Michigan, he drove 15 of them into his house and played his guitar to them.

Paul Scarron (1610–60)

French poet. Scarron wrote numerous sonnets, songs and satires but is best known for his novel *Le Roman Comique* (The Comic Novel). He was once married to Madame de Maintenon (the second wife of LOUIS XIV) and dedicated a book of his poems to his sister's female dog. However, while the book was being printed they had an argument and an erratum slip was later added: 'For "my sister's bitch" read "my bitch of a sister".'

William Shenstone (1714–63)

British poet and landscape gardener. Best known for his poem *The Schoolmistress* (1742), Shenstone had a dog called Lucy which features in a painting of him by Edward Alcock.

Dame Edith Sitwell (1887–1964)

British poet. When living in Paris this eccentric Englishwoman owned a cat of which she was very fond. She even bought it a record – 'Baby Don't Be Blue' – adding 'My cat had a passion for this song ...' Once asked how to tell good poetry from bad she replied, 'In the same way as you can tell fish ... if it's fresh it's good, if it's stale it's bad, and if you're not certain, try it on the cat.'

As a child she had a peacock called Peaky, a puffin with a wooden leg and a baby owl that had fallen out of its nest, which she says in her autobiography, *Taken Care Of*, used 'to sleep with its head on its shoulder, pretending to snore in order to attract mice'. In the 1960s she lived in a flat in Hampstead, London, with four cats: Orion, Belaker, a Siamese called Shadow and the cream-coloured Leo (her favourite, photographed with her by Mark Gerson in 1962).

Christopher Smart (1722–71)

British poet. This eighteenth-century British poet, whose best-known work is *A Song to David* (1763) – written soon after leaving a mental asylum in London – wrote a long poem about his cat Jeoffry, which begins:

For I will consider my cat Jeoffry.

For he is the servant of the Living God, duly and daily serving him

For the first glance of the glory of God in the East he worships in his way. [...]

For having done duty and received blessing he begins to consider himself.

For this he performs in ten degrees.

For first he looks upon his forepaws to see if they are clean.

For secondly he kicks up behind to clear away there.

For thirdly he works it upon stretch with the forepaws extended.

For fourthly he sharpens his paws by wood.

For fifthly he washes himself.

For sixthly he rolls upon wash.

For seventhly he fleas himself, that he may not be interrupted upon the beat.

For eighthly he rubs himself against a post.

For ninethly he looks up for his instructions.

For tenthly he goes in quest of food.

For having consider'd God and himself he consider his neighbour.

For if he meets another cat he will kiss her in kindness.

Robert Southey (1774–1843)

British poet and historian. Southey, who was elected Poet Laureate in 1813, kept more than 12 cats at his home, Greta Hall, in Keswick in the Lake District. These included Bona Marietta and Lord Nelson ('an ugly specimen of the streaked carrotty, or Judas-coloured kind') – both of whom were named by his seven-year-old nephew, Hartley Coleridge (the son of the poet SAMUEL TAYLOR COLERIDGE) – The Zombi and Sir Thomas Dido (a dark tabby originally thought to be female and called just Dido). Bona Fidelia was a tortoiseshell daughter of Lord Nelson who had a surviving daughter Madame Bianchi and a granddaughter, Pulcheria. One that stands out from the others because of its name was a tabby-and-white cat with green eyes called His Serene Highness, the Archduke Rumpelstilzchen, Marquis Macbum, Earl Tomlemange, Baron Raticide, Waouhler and Skaratsch. It was given the first of its names after it appeared one day just as the poet had finished reading the story of Rumpelstiltskin to his children. Rumpel's arch-enemy was Hurlyburlybuss who was master of the garden. But on one occasion they met without incident:

Some weeks ago Hurlyburlybuss was manifestly emaciated and enfeebled by ill health, and Rumpelstilzchen with great magnanimity made overtures of peace. The whole progress of the treaty was seen from the parlour window. The caution with which Rumpel made his advances, the sullen dignity with which they were received, their mutual uneasiness when Rumpel, after slow and wary approach, seated himself whisker-to-whisker with his rival, the mutual fear which restrained not only teeth and claws, but even all tones of defiance, the mutual agitation of their tails which, though they did not expand with anger, could not be kept still for suspense, and lastly the manner in which Hurly retreated, like Ajax still keeping his face towards his old antagonist, were worthy to have been represented by that painter who was called the Rafaelle of Cats. The overture I fear was not accepted as generously as it was made; for no sooner had Hurlyburlybuss recovered strength than hostilities were recommenced with greater violence than ever ...

It was Southey who declared that 'A kitten is in the animal world what a rosebud is in the garden.'

A.C. Swinburne (1837–1909)

British poet. Swinburne first achieved fame with his play *Atalanta in Calydon* (1865) and his *Poems and Ballads* published the same year. A friend of DANTE GABRIEL ROSSETTI, he was very fond of cats and wrote a poem to one of his pets, 'a friend of loftier mind', which begins:

> Stately, kindly, lordly friend,
> > Condescend
> Here to sit by me, and turn
> Glorious eyes that smile and burn,
> Golden eyes, love's lustrous meed,
> On the golden page I read. [...]
>
> Dogs may fawn on all and some,
> > As they come;
> You, a friend of loftier mind,
> Answer friends alone in kind;
> Just your foot upon my hand
> Softly bids it understand.

Torquato Tasso (1544–95)

Italian poet. This famous Italian Renaissance poet, who is best known for his epic work about the First Crusade, *Jerusalem Liberated* (1581), wrote a poem 'Sonnet to my Cats' about his pets, which included one called Massara.

Alfred Lord Tennyson (1809–92)

British poet. Tennyson was created Poet Laureate in 1850, the same year that his famous poem 'In Memoriam' was published. He is also famed for such poems as 'The Lady of Shallot', 'The Lotus-eaters', *Maud* and *Idylls of the King*. When living on the Isle of Wight he had a pony called Fanny who used to pull his wife Emily about in a wheelchair. He also had a dog called Old Don.

Virgil (70–19 BC)

Roman poet. The story has it that the great Roman poet who wrote the *Aeneid* amongst other works, had a pet fly. When it died Virgil gave the insect a lavish funeral at his home on the Esquiline Hill in Rome, a highlight of which was the oration, which was given by Virgil's patron, the politician Maecenas.

John Greenleaf Whittier (1807–92)

US poet and writer. Whittier helped to found the magazine *Atlantic Monthly* and is best known for such poems as 'The Barefoot Boy' and the collection *Snow-Bound* (1866). He also had a cat called Bathsheba whom he commemorated in a short poem of the same name when she died:

> To whom none ever said scat,
> No worthier cat
> Ever sat on a mat
> Or caught a rat:
> Resquies – cat.

William Wordsworth (1770–1850)

British poet. Wordsworth, who was famed for such poems as 'Tintern Abbey' and *The Prelude*, owned a dog that reputedly raised its hackles and barked if the poet wrote something that had the wrong rhythm when it was read out. Wordsworth also wrote two poems about a greyhound bitch called Music which was owned by his brother-in-law Thomas Hutchinson. 'Incident Characteristic of a Favourite Dog' (1805) described how she fell into a well and 'Tribute to the Memory of the Same Dog' (1805) was written when she died.

Sir Thomas Wyatt (1503–42)

British poet and diplomat. Without the help of an unnamed cat who helped save the life of Wyatt's father, SIR HENRY WYATT, it is doubtful whether the famous Renaissance poet and friend of ANNE BOLEYN would have been born. Sir Henry had been imprisoned in the Tower of London by RICHARD III, tortured and denied all food. However, this heroic cat somehow managed to bring Wyatt a number of pigeons to eat in his cell which allowed him to survive long enough for Henry VII to accede to the throne, after which he was released. His son Thomas was conceived after he left the Tower.

W.B. Yeats (1865–1939)

Irish poet and playwright. Yeats was awarded the Nobel Prize for Literature in 1923 and was also a senator of the Irish Free State (1922–28). His inspiration Maud Gonne, for whom he had an unrequited love, owned a grey marmoset called Chaperone which she bought in Marseilles in 1887 when she was 20 and travelling alone to Constantinople. Chaperone later died of the cold in St Petersburg when accompanying Gonne on a journey from Paris to Russia.

Politics & Military Affairs

John Quincy Adams (1767–1848)

Sixth US President. Adams, who was the son of John Adams, the second US President, became President himself in 1825, and died after suffering a stroke while giving a speech in Congress. When President he kept silk worms. He also had an alligator, which was a present from the Marquis de Lafayette – the French nobleman who had fought against the British during the War of Independence and was a friend of GEORGE WASHINGTON – and kept it in the East Room of the White House.

Alcibiades (c. 450–404 BC)

Athenian general and politician. Alcibiades was a pupil of the great Greek philosopher Socrates (as was Plato, who includes Alcibiades in his *Symposium*). In addition he was brought up by the great Greek general Pericles and succeeded him after his death. Alcibiades had a famous dog which is described in Plutarch's *Parallel Lives* as having a very large tail. One day, when Alcibiades was in bad favour (he was later murdered) he had the dog's tail cut off so that the people would talk about the dog rather than about his own exploits.

Robert Baden-Powell (1857–1941)

British general. Famed as the defender of Mafeking during the Boer War and as the founder of the Boy Scouts in 1908, Baden-Powell had two Labrador dogs and kept ponies for his children to ride. In addition he had a pet hyrax (a small, nocturnal, rabbit-like mammal) called Hyrie.

Prince Otto von Bismarck (1815–98)

First Chancellor of Germany. Prime Minister of Prussia under Wilhem I, Bismarck came to fame as the 'Iron Chancellor' and the unifier of Germany in the 19th century after the defeat of France in the Franco-Prussian War (1871). A great dog-lover, two of his black Great Danes were called Tyras. The first of these was his companion at the University of Göttingen when he was a student (he studied law and agriculture) and the latter he owned in his old age. Kaiser Wilhelm II also sent him a small dog in 1888.

Martin van Buren (1782–1862)

Eighth US President. Van Buren, who was known as the 'Little Magician' because of his wily ways and political astuteness (and also because he was only 5 feet 6 inches tall), became President in 1836. The expression OK is supposed to have originated during his term in office, and stands for Old Kinderhook, a nickname for Van Buren which alluded to his birthplace in Kinderhook, New York. When President he kept two tiger cubs which were a present from the Sultan of Oman, but later gave them to a zoo.

George Canning (1770–1827)

British statesman and poet. Canning became Foreign Secretary when Castlereagh committed suicide in 1822 and briefly Prime Minister in 1827. An accomplished poet, he even wrote verse in honour of his cat.

Nicolae Ceaucescu (1918–89)

Romanian President. During his presidency (1967-89) Ceaucescu owned a dog called Corbu which he gave the rank of colonel. The dog features in the play, *The Final Interrogation of Ceaucescu's Dog*, by Warren Leight.

Sir Winston Churchill (1874–1965)

British statesman. Churchill owned a green budgerigar called Toby and two poodles, Rufus I and Rufus II. No one ate before the dogs had been fed. He also kept a number of cats, including a black stray Margate (named after his speech to the Conservative Party on 10 October 1953, in Margate, Kent, which was the day the kitten arrived at No. 10), and three ginger cats, Jock, Tango and Ginger. Tango, a marmalade tom, was drawn by the celebrated artist Sir William Nicholson (who himself owned four cats). During the war years one of Churchill's ministers visited him when he was laid up with 'flu at Chequers and entered his room to find the great statesman in bed with his large black cat Nelson purring contentedly on his feet. Seeing the minister's expression, Churchill announced, 'This cat does more for the war effort than you do. He acts as a hot-water bottle and saves fuel and power.'

El Cid (*c.* 1030–99)

Spanish general. The hero of the long 12th-century Spanish national epic, *Poema del Cid* was the Castilian nobleman Rodrigo Diaz de Bivar, el Cid Campeador (the lord and champion) who rose to fame in the battles with the Moors and with King Sancho of Navarre. The Cid's famous horse, Babieca, was a gift from his godfather. The story goes that when asked which horse he would like, the Cid chose the most plain and immature of those offered. His godfather's response was 'babieca!' which means 'stupid' or 'simpleton' in Spanish, and the name stuck. When the Cid was dying in 1099 his last wish was that his body, in full armour and with sword raised, should be strapped to Babieca and sent into battle. The effect was dramatic – the Moors, seeing him leading his troops, thought he had been reincarnated and fled the battlefield.

After El Cid died, Babieca was never ridden again and eventually died himself two years later aged 40. The horse was buried in front of the gate of the monastery of Valencia and two elm trees were planted to mark the site.

Alan Clark (1928–99)

British politician and historian. The notorious Tory politician had a tame jackdaw called Max which the family had reared from a chick when it fell from its nest. After being released back into the wild he would regularly come to the window of their house. In his *Diary* for 1983 Clark said: 'Max carries a lot of my good luck with him' and he would worry if the bird disappeared for any length of time. Clark also owned a number of dogs, including a Jack Russell terrier called Tom. White, black and brown, Tom had a white face with brown ears. Clark said that after he died people could say that he had 'gone to join Tom and the other dogs'. He was buried at his home, Saltwood

Castle in Kent, alongside two of his dogs, the Labrador Gussy and the Rottweiler Eva Braun.

Georges Clemenceau (1841–1929)

French statesman. Clemenceau, nicknamed the Tiger, was twice Prime Minister of France and negotiated the Treaty of Versailles after the First World War. He had a black cat called Prudence.

Calvin Coolidge (1872–1933)

Thirtieth US President. President Coolidge had a white collie dog called Rob Roy. Presented as a gift in 1923 it was originally named Oshkosh but was renamed by Grace Coolidge. In the portrait by Howard Chandler Christy in the White House, the dog is Rob Roy (though Mrs Coolidge also had her own white collie, a bitch called Prudence Prim). Rob Roy died in 1928 and was replaced by a brown-and-white spotted Shetland sheepdog from Michigan originally called Diana of Wildwood. Mrs Coolidge renamed her Calamity Jane after she arrived by aeroplane covered in grease. In 1923 he was also present-ed with an Airedale called Laddie Buck, a half-brother of Laddie Boy whom he had inherited from his predecessor, President Harding. Mrs Coolidge renamed him Paul Pry because he was always sniffing around.

When President (1923–9) Coolidge also had a grey-striped cat called Tiger and two others named Blackie and Timmie. In addition he had a canary called Caruso (and three others called Nip, Tuck and Snowflake) and a pet racoon called Rebecca. The racoon had been sent to him from friends in Mississippi as a gift for Thanksgiving dinner but instead of eating her he kept her in a pen and took her for walks on a lead. He later got a male racoon, Horace, to keep her company.

Other pets included a Chow called Blackberry (and another called Tiny Tim), a bulldog called Boston Beans, a yellow collie called Bessie, a brown collie called Ruby Rough, two dogs called King Kole and Palo Alto, a terrier called Peter Pan, a thrush called Old Bill and a goose called Enoch.

Oliver Cromwell (1599–1658)

British soldier and statesman. The MP for Cambridge and a staunch Puritan, it was Cromwell's 'Ironsides' and New Model Army that helped defeat CHARLES I in the English Civil War. After Charles's execution Cromwell became the ruler of England though he refused the crown in 1657. The Cromwell family kept a pet monkey and the story goes that when Oliver was a baby in Huntingdon this monkey snatched him from his cradle and carried him up to the top of the roof, from which he was rescued only with great difficulty.

Cromwell also owned a greyhound called Coffin-Nail.

Dwight D. Eisenhower (1890–1969)

Thirty-fourth US President. When Supreme Commander in the Second World War General Eisenhower had a black kitten called Shaef in his headquarters at Sharpener

Camp, England (SHAEF stood for Supreme Headquarters Allied Expeditionary Force). However, when President (1953–61) and living at the White House he was not fond of cats and told his staff to shoot any they saw. He also had a Weimaraner dog called Heidi.

James Garfield (1831–81)
Twentieth US President. Garfield was one of the shortest-serving Presidents of the USA (March–September 1881), being assassinated soon after coming into office. He had a mare called Kit and a dog called Veto.

William Ewart Gladstone (1809–98)
British statesman and Prime Minister. Gladstone kept a number of dogs including a black Pomeranian called Petz who was later buried in the dog cemetery at Hawarden Park near Hawarden Castle, Flintshire, Wales (owned by his brother-in-law Sir Stephen Glynne and Gladstone's home in his later years).

Ulysses S. Grant (1822–85)
Eighteenth US President. The General's favourite mount during the American Civil War was Cincinnatus, a gift from the people of Cincinnati, Ohio. Grant took the horse with him to Washington when he became President in 1869. Other horses he owned included Egypt, St Louis, Julia, Reb, Billy Button and the Shetland ponies Jennie and Mary. He also had a Newfoundland dog called Faithful.

Warren G. Harding (1865–1923)

Twenty-eighth US President. The first gift former newspaper publisher Harding received when he became President of the USA in 1921 was an Airedale puppy called Laddie Boy (originally Caswell Laddie Boy). A fond pet, when the President died he was inherited by his successor, CALVIN COOLIDGE. As a tribute, newspaper sellers all over the USA donated pennies for a statuette of the dog to be presented to Mrs Harding but unfortunately she died before it was made and it now resides in the Smithsonian Institution. He also received a white English bulldog called Oh Boy.

Benjamin Harrison (1833–1901)

Twenty-third US President. Elected in 1888, Harrison was the grandson of WILLIAM HENRY HARRISON, the ninth US President. During his term of office six new states joined the USA – North Dakota, South Dakota, Washington, Montana, Idaho and Wyoming. He kept a billy goat called Old Whiskers.

William Henry Harrison (1773–1841)

Ninth US President. The son of one of the signatories of the Declaration of Independence and himself a brigadier-general in the war against Britain in 1812, Harrison was the first US president to die in office. Elected in 1841 he died of pneumonia a month after his inauguration. Harrison kept a goat and a cow called Sukey.

Rutherford B. Hayes (1822–93)

Nineteenth US President. President Hayes owned the first-ever Siamese cat in the USA, called Siam. Sent to his wife, Lucy, in 1878 by the American consul in Bangkok the cat died a year later and was stuffed. He also had a greyhound called Grim, an English mastiff called Duke, a Newfoundland called Hector and a terrier called Dot.

Paul von Hindenburg (1847–1934)

German General and President. Hindenburg became a general in 1903 and retired in 1911 but was recalled during the First World War. He became the second president of the German Republic in 1925, was re-elected in 1932, and in 1933 appointed Hitler as Chancellor. Hindenburg owned a number of cats and once said: 'I cannot imagine a pleasant retired life of peace and meditation without a cat in the house.'

Adolf Hitler (1889–1945)

Austrian-born German dictator. While serving on the Western Front in the First World War Hitler kept a small dog called Fuchsl which he trained to walk up and down ladders (it was stolen in 1917). He later kept Alsatians, including Wolf and a female, Blondi, who was a gift from Martin Bormann. Though Blondi accompanied Hitler on many important missions she often had to be shut away at Berchtesgaden as she would fight with Eva Braun's two Scotties. Hitler trained Blondi to perform many tricks including jumping hoops, climbing a ladder, jumping over walls and begging, and she would even 'sing' when Hitler praised her. When Hitler was contemplating suicide for himself and Eva Braun in the bunker in Berlin he tested out the cyanide on Blondi first – it worked. Hitler also reputedly hated cats.

Herbert Hoover (1874–1964)

Thirty-first US President. It is said that a photograph of Hoover with his dog King Tut helped gain him the Presidency of the United States in 1928. He had acquired the dog in 1917 when organising war relief in Belgium. He also had two fox terriers – Big Ben and Sonnie – a setter called Eaglehurst Gilette, a Scotch collie called Glen, an elkhound called Weejie, a wolfhound called Patrick and an Eskimo dog called Yukon.

J. Edgar Hoover (1895–1972)

US civil servant. Hoover became Director of the Federal Bureau of Investigation in 1924 and remained in control of it for nearly 50 years until his death. He owned a dog called Spee De Bozo.

Andrew Jackson (1767–1845)

Seventh US President. Nicknamed 'Old Hickory', Jackson kept white mice and a parrot called Pol. He also had a number of horses: Truxton, Sam Patch, Emily, Lady Nashville and Bolivia. Jackson's statue in Lafayette Park was the first equestrian statue of an American to be erected in the USA.

Thomas J. 'Stonewall' Jackson (1824–63)

US general. Jackson's favourite mount was a gelding called Little Sorrel. Unfortunately it led to the Confederate general's death when on 2 May 1863 he rode the horse into the woods near Chancellorsville, Virginia, to reconnoitre the position of the Union troops stationed there. By mistake he was shot and badly injured by his own troops and the horse panicked and bolted. Eventually the horse was caught but eight days later the general died. Little Sorrel himself died in 1886 and his stuffed hide can be seen in the Virginia Military Institute in Lexington.

Thomas Jefferson (1743–1826)

Third US President. Jefferson was a cat-lover but the first US President to bring a cat into the White House was ABRAHAM LINCOLN. Jefferson was also a keen horseman and always rode for two to three hours every day. He was so fussy about the cleanliness of his horses that when one was brought to him for his daily ride he would wipe a white handkerchief across its back and if there was any dirt on it would send it back to the stables for further grooming. He also kept a mocking-bird when living in the White House, a present from General Lafayette.

Lyndon B. Johnson (1908–73)

Thirty-sixth US President. President Johnson had a white collie dog called Blanco which shook hands with its paw. He also had a pair of beagles, Him and Her, when he moved into the White House in 1963. Both died unnatural deaths, Her dying in 1964 after swallowing a stone and Him being run over by a car while chasing a squirrel in 1966. Soon after this Johnson adopted a white mongrel called Yuki ('snow' in Japanese) which his daughter Luci had found abandoned at a filling station.

John F. Kennedy (1917–63)

Thirty-fifth US President. In 1961 Soviet Premier Nikita Khrushchev presented President Kennedy's wife, Jacqueline with a six-month-old puppy, Pushinka (Russian for 'fluffy'), which was one of a litter produced by Strelka, a female Samoyed husky dog who was (with Belka, a similar dog) the first animal to survive an orbital flight in space. Strelka and Belka were launched in *Sputnik V* by the Soviet Union on 19 August 1960 and completed 17 orbits in 25 hours. Jackie also had a German shepherd dog called Clipper given her by her father-in-law Joseph Kennedy and in addition was given a bay gelding horse called Sardar by President Khan of Pakistan during her 1962 visit to the country.

When Kennedy died, a riderless 16-year-old chestnut

military ceremonial horse called Black Jack was led behind his coffin from the Capitol to St Matthew's Church and then on to Arlington Cemetery. The horse carried a sheathed sword strapped to its saddle and had boots reversed in its stirrups as a symbol that a leader had fallen and would ride no more.

Kennedy also owned a black-and-white mongrel dog called Friday and a piebald pony called Macaroni who was the special pet of his daughter Caroline. A New York composer was even inspired to write a song about the horse called 'My Pony, Macaroni'. Caroline also had a Welsh terrier, Charlie, who sired four puppies with Pushinka, and a blue-grey shorthaired cat called Tom Kitten, named after the BEATRIX POTTER character.

Other pets in the Kennedy household included a rabbit (Zsa Zsa), two ponies (Tex and Leprechaun), two parakeets (Bluebell and Marybelle), two hamsters (Debbie and Billie), a canary (Robin) and a mongrel dog called Wolf. In addition JFK had an Irish cocker spaniel called Shannon which was given him by Irish Prime Minister Eamon de Valera.

Robert Kennedy (1925–68)

US politician. The younger brother of US President JOHN F. KENNEDY, Bobby Kennedy was Attorney General (1961–64) and senator for New York, and had been elected as a candidate for US president when he was assassinated in Los Angeles. He owned a Newfoundland dog called Brumis.

T.E. Lawrence (1888–1935)

British writer and military leader. 'Lawrence of Arabia' was famed for his military exploits with Britain's Arab allies fighting against the Turks in the desert during the First World War and for his book *The Seven Pillars of Wisdom* (1926). He also kept a female racing camel called Naama which he accidentally shot in action near Akaba.

Robert E. Lee (1807–70)

US general. Lee is perhaps best known as the Commander-in-Chief of the Confederate Army in the American Civil War. However, during the Mexican War (1846) he was chief engineer of the army and owned a cat which had been sent to him by his daughter.

Abraham Lincoln (1809–65)

Sixteenth US President. Lincoln owned a yellow mongrel dog called Fido when living in Springfield, Illinois, before he was elected President. When the family moved to Washington in 1861 the dog was left behind with neighbours and it was later stabbed to death by a drunk. Lincoln also owned a stray dog called Jip and two goats, Nanko and Nanny, which he bought for his ten-year-old son Tad. They had to live in the White House itself as the gardener complained of their chewing up the flowers.

The Lincolns also owned pigs, turkeys and a number of cats including one called Tabby. In addition there is a story that while visiting General Grant's headquarters during the American Civil War Lincoln rescued three

kittens which later lived in the White House – the first cats ever to do so. Lincoln also famously said: 'No matter how much cats fight, there always seem to be plenty of kittens.'

Ramsay MacDonald (1866–1937)
British statesman and Prime Minister. When a young man and working at a London post office, the future Labour PM had an encounter with a cat that changed his life. The black cat which was a pet at the sorting office had been trained to lick stamps and, to wish him luck, MacDonald got the cat to lick the stamp for a letter he was sending to *The Times*. The letter was published and MacDonald's career began in earnest.

William McKinley (1843–1901)

Twenty-fifth US President. Elected in 1896 and returned for a second term in 1900, McKinley was shot shortly afterwards by an anarchist in Buffalo. Among his pets was a Mexican parrot.

Sir Thomas More (1478–1535)

British statesman. Sir Thomas More became Lord Chancellor under HENRY VIII and was also an important scholar, writing among other books the influential *Utopia* (1516). When living in Chelsea, More kept an aviary, a small dog and a pet monkey (which featured in Holbein's portrait of him).

Benito Mussolini (1883–1945)

Italian dictator. After the famous March on Rome of his Fascist Party in 1922, Mussolini became Prime Minister of Italy and remained dictator of the country until he was deposed in 1943. Known as 'Il Duce' ('The Leader'), he was a keen horseman and also owned a Persian cat.

Horatio, Viscount Nelson (1758–1805)

British admiral. Nelson had a cat called Tiddles which was present on HMS *Victory* at the Battle of Trafalgar. Originally a pet of Emma Hamilton and discovered as a stray kitten in the courtyard of the British Embassy in Naples in 1797, she returned with the Hamiltons to England in 1800 and was presented to Nelson by Emma

in 1803. After the death of Nelson Tiddles was trans-
ferred to HMS *Amphion* and eventually died at the siege
of Trieste in 1813.

Richard Nixon (1913–94)

Thirty-seventh US President. When standing for election
as Vice-President of the USA in 1952 Nixon owned a
black-and-white spotted cocker spaniel called Checkers. It
was named by Nixon's six-year-old daughter Tricia. The
dog became famous when Senator Nixon was accused of
receiving secret financial gifts to the value of $18,000
during the election. He claimed that there was no impro-
priety and said that he had also received the dog as a gift
from an admirer in Texas and that as his kids loved the
dog there was no way he was going to give it back. This
moving performance on TV was later called the Checkers
Speech. Another dog owned by Nixon was an Irish setter
called King Timahoe, which was a present from his New
York campaign staff in 1969. Nixon named it after the
village in Ireland where his mother's ancestors came
from. He also had a French poodle called Vicky and a
Yorkshire terrier named Pasha.

George Patton (1885–1945)

US general. This flamboyant US general, who led the US
7th Army in the Sicily landings in 1943 and commanded
the US 3rd Army during the invasion of France in 1944,
was killed in a motoring accident at the end of the Second
World War. He owned a white bull terrier dog called
William the Conqueror.

Manfred von Richthofen (1882–1918)

German aviator. The Bloody Red Baron was the highest scoring air ace on either side in the First World War, with a total of 80 Allied aircraft shot down. A very reserved and aloof character, he rarely smiled and, though he was greatly admired – even idolised – by his colleagues, he had very few close friends. He also had great difficulty relaxing and his only real love was his dog. He once said 'The most beautiful thing in all creation is my Danish hound, Moritz.' The brindled dog slept on his bed and even on occasion flew with him. On one of these forays into the air Richthofen reported that Moritz 'quite enjoyed himself and looked about intelligently'.

Maximilien Robespierre (1758–94)

French revolutionary leader. Known as 'the Incorruptible', Robespierre introduced the Reign of Terror during the French Revolution which led to the guillotining of many members of the nobility. He kept pigeons all his life and also owned a number of canaries.

Franklin Delano Roosevelt (1884–1945)

Thirty-second US President. President Roosevelt had a Scotty dog called Fala who in 1945 got into a fight with Blaze a bull mastiff owned by his son, Elliott. Fala was badly hurt and Blaze had to be put down. Fala was originally named Big Boy when he was given to the President by his cousin Margaret Stuckley in 1940 and Roosevelt renamed him Murray the Outlaw of Fala Hill, shortened to Fala, in honour of a Scottish ancestor. Fala slept in the President's bedroom and was with Roosevelt when he met Churchill on the USS *Augusta* in 1941. When the president died at Warm Springs, Georgia, in April 1945 Fala jumped up and, barking loudly, ran up a hill and refused to come down. Nonetheless he lived for a further seven years, looked after by Eleanor Roosevelt who also had a dog called Gems.

Other pets included a German Shepherd dog called Major, a Great Dane called President, an English Sheepdog called Tiny, a Llewellyn Setter called Winks, a female Scottish terrier called Meggie (which once bit a senator) and two other dogs – Mr Marksman and Medworth.

Theodore Roosevelt (1858–1919)

Twenty-sixth US President. When Theodore Roosevelt was President of the United States the unquestioned master of the White House was his six-toed grey cat, Slippers, so named because of his larger than usual feet. Whenever a diplomatic dinner or summit conference was held Slippers would make sure he was always the centre of attention, to such a degree that on one occasion in 1906 he even blocked the access to a banquet by sprawling across a rug in the entrance – the President, his aides and international ambassadors from every corner of the globe had to walk around him. Frequently absent for days and even weeks on end, Slippers had remarkably prescient powers and always returned home when a high-level meeting was imminent. Indeed, so reliable a guide were his movements to the goings on at the White House that journalists would eagerly await the cat's reappearance in the grounds as a harbinger of major events.

Roosevelt also had a cat called Tom Quartz – named after the cat in Mark Twain's *Roughing It* – who later became the subject of a biography, establishing a tradition of presidential pet memoirs. As a kitten, Tom was always teasing their long-suffering dog Jack, as Roosevelt described in a letter:

> Tom Quartz is certainly the cunningest kitten I have ever seen. He is always playing pranks on Jack and I get very nervous lest Jack should grow too irritated. The other evening they were both in the library – Jack sleeping before the fire – Tom Quartz scampering about, an exceedingly playful creature – which is about what he is. He would race across the floor, then jump upon the curtain or play with the tassel. Suddenly he spied Jack and galloped up to him. Jack, looking exceedingly sullen and shame-faced, jumped out of the way and got upon the sofa and around the table, and Tom Quartz instantly jumped upon him again. Jack suddenly shifted to the other sofa, where Tom Quartz again went after him. Then Jack started for the door, while Tom made a rapid turn under the sofa and around the table and just as Jack reached the door leaped on his hind-quarters. Jack bounded forward and away and the two went tandem out of the room – Jack not co-operating at all; and about five minutes afterwards Tom Quartz stalked solemnly back.

Roosevelt also owned an Icelandic pony called Algonquin and a small black mongrel dog, Skip, which would jump up on the pony's back and ride along with him. The favourite pet of Roosevelt's son Archibald, the boy would often ride the pony to school. The family also had a spaniel called Manchu, a Chesapeake Retriever called Sailor Boy and two other dogs – Scamp and Pete.

The teddy bear came about as a result of Roosevelt's fondness for shooting bears. While in Mississippi in 1902 to settle a boundary dispute Roosevelt refused to shoot a bearcub and this later appeared as a cartoon by Clifford Berryman 'Drawing the Line in Mississippi', published in the *Washington Star* on 18 November 1902. The owner of a candy store in Brooklyn then made a bear doll based on the cartoon and called it Teddy's Bear. The bears sold quickly and the owner of the store, Morris Michtom, founded the Ideal Toy Corporation. He sent a bear to Roosevelt himself which is now in the Smithsonian Institution in Washington DC.

Horses owned by Roosevelt included Renown, Roswell, Rusty, Jocko, Root, Grey, Dawn, Wyoming, Yangenka and his favourite, Bleistein. He also kept two carriage horses – General and Judge.

Other pets in the Roosevelt household included a number of guinea-pigs – Dewey Senior, Dewey Junior, Bob Evans, Bishop Doan and Father O'Grady – as well as a macaw (Eli), a piebald rat (Jonathan) and a garter snake (Emily Spinach).

William Howard Taft (1857–1930)
Twenty-seventh US President. When Taft was President of the USA (1909–13) he had a Holstein cow called Pauline Wayne. She was the last of a long line of cows that were allowed to graze on the White House lawn to provide milk for the families of presidents.

Zachary Taylor (1784–1850)
Twelfth US President. Before he became President of the USA in 1849, General Taylor rode to battle in the Mexican wars on a knock-kneed horse called Old Whitey. After he entered the White House, the horse was allowed to graze on its lawns.

Harry S. Truman (1884–1972)
Thirty-third US President. Truman, who came to power on the death of FRANKLIN DELANO ROOSEVELT in 1945, was responsible for the dropping of two atomic

bombs on Japan and the sending of US troops to South Korea. He owned a dog called Feller and an Irish setter called Mike.

John Tyler (1790–1862)
Tenth US President. John Tyler's period as President of the United States of America (1841–45) saw the annexation of the state of Texas and the reorganisation of the US Navy. While President, Tyler had a favourite horse called The General. When it died it was buried in Sherwood, Virginia. He also owned a greyhound called Le Beau.

Sir Robert Walpole (1676–1745)
British Prime Minister. Walpole was the leading minister of GEORGE I and GEORGE II and is generally acknowledged as being the first British Prime Minister, though he personally disliked the term. He owned an Italian hound called Patapan which appears in his portrait by John Wootton.

George Washington (1732–99)
First President of the USA. Thomas Nelson, Governor of Virginia, gave Washington a three-year-old chestnut gelding in 1765 and for ten years the horse, named Nelson by Washington, was his favourite mount. He rode the horse to Philadelphia to accept command of the Continental Army in 1775 in the USA's revolution against British rule,

and also took him to Yorktown in 1781 for the British surrender. After retiring to Mount Vernon, Washington never rode the horse again. Washington was also the first breeder of mules and American jackasses in the USA. The first one to join his stud farm in Mount Vernon and sire a mule was a grey Catalonian donkey (or jackass) called Royal Gift, presented by King Charles III of Spain in 1785.

Other pets included the dogs Vulcan, Taster, Tipler, Searcher, Sweetlips (a foxhound), Mopsy, Forester, Captain, Chloe and Lady Rover. He also owned cats, though the first US President to bring a cat into the White House was ABRAHAM LINCOLN. Another pet was a parrot called Polly and a Dalmatian dog called Madam Moos who was the particular pet of his wife.

Arthur Wellesley, 1st Duke of Wellington
(1769–1852)
British general and statesman. Wellington's favourite mount was the chestnut stallion Copenhagen. The grandson of the famous racehorse Eclipse, Wellington bought the horse aged four in 1812 at the start of the Peninsular wars against Napoleon. The Iron Duke rode the horse into battle at Waterloo and he was later retired to the Duke's estate at Strathfield Saye where he died in 1836. Wellington also had a terrier dog called Vic when studying at a military college in Angers, France, and later had a white terrier called Jack.

Harold Wilson (1916–95)

British Prime Minister. Harold Wilson owned a Siamese cat called Nemo. The resident cat at No. 10 Downing Street during the reigns of Wilson, Heath, Callaghan and Thatcher was called Wilberforce. Mainly white with patches of tabby and black, Wilberforce was originally a gift from the RSPCA to Prime Minister Edward Heath in 1973. He retired in 1988 and died two years later.

Woodrow Wilson (1856–1924)

Twenty-eighth US President. Famed for his peace plans for the Versailles conference after the First World War – which gained him the Nobel Peace Prize in 1919 – and for his championship of the League of Nations, Wilson had an Airedale dog called Dance. Not everyone approved of Wilson's political views – DOROTHY PARKER named one of her dogs Woodrow Wilson 'because it was full of shit'. Wilson also owned a ram called Old Ike.

Sir Henry Wyatt (1460–1537)

British statesman. Sir Henry Wyatt was a supporter of the Lancastrian party in the Wars of the Roses and was imprisoned and tortured by RICHARD III. Later released by Henry VII, he held high office and became the father of the famous poet and statesman SIR THOMAS WYATT. However, had it not been for the good offices of a cat who became his pet in the Tower of London, Wyatt would certainly have perished of starvation. The naturalist W.H. Hudson recounted the story in his book *A Shepherd's Life* (1910):

> And here I recall an old story of a cat (an immortal puss) who only hunted pigeons. This tells that Sir Henry Wyatt was imprisoned in the Tower of London by Richard III, and was cruelly treated, having no bed to sleep on in his cell and scarcely food enough to keep him alive. One winter night, when he was half-dead with cold, a cat appeared in his cell, having come down the chimney, and was very friendly, and slept curled up on his chest, thus keeping him warm all night. In the morning it vanished up the chimney, but appeared later with a pigeon, which it gave to Sir Henry, and then again departed. When the jailer appeared and repeated that he durst not bring more than the few morsels of food provided, Sir Henry then asked: 'Wilt thou dress any I provide?' This the jailer promised to do, for he pitied his prisoner, and taking the pigeon had it dressed and cooked for him. The cat continued bringing pigeons every day, and the jailer, thinking they were sent miraculously, continued to cook them, so that Sir Henry fared well, despite the order which Richard gave later, that no food at all was to be provided. He was getting impatient of his prisoner's power to keep alive on very little food, and he didn't want to behead him – he wanted him to die naturally. Thus in the end Sir Henry outlived the tyrant and was set free, and the family preserve the story to this day. It is classed as folklore, but there is no reason to prevent one from accepting it as literal truth.

Music & Entertainment

Fred Astaire (1899–1987)

US dancer, singer and actor. Born Frederick Austerlitz, Astaire was best known for his tap-dancing routines with Ginger Rogers in such films as *Top Hat* (1935) and *Swing Time* (1936). After retiring in 1946 he returned to great success in *Easter Parade* (1948) and other films. He was also a great animal lover and owned dogs, horses and cats including a white female that just disappeared one day without a trace and a black female which lived in the stables with the horses and which must have been very popular with the neighbourhood toms as it once gave birth to a litter that included ginger, grey, black and tabby kittens!

Mary Astor (1906–87)

US actress. Born Lucile Vasconcells Langhanke, the daughter of a German teacher, Mary Astor was the beautiful star of silent films such as *Beau Brummell* (1924) and *Don Juan* (1926) – both with John Barrymore – and won an Oscar for *The Great Lie* in 1941. She was also devoted to cats and owned a number of Siamese which she wrote about in a book, *My Friends Have Blue Eyes*.

Hermione Baddeley (1908–89)

British actress. Hermione Baddeley appeared in many TV, film and theatre productions and was nominated for an Oscar as Best Supporting Actress for her part in *Room at the Top* (1959). She also played Sister George in Frank

Marcus's play *The Killing of Sister George* (later made into a film starring BERYL REID). She dedicated her book *The Unsinkable Hermione Baddeley* (1984) to her pet George, 'my wonderful French bulldog', who was named after the character.

George Balanchine (1904–83)

US choreographer. Born in St Petersburg, Russia, as George Melitonovich Balanchivadze, Balanchine founded the Ballet Russes de Monte Carlo and later moved to the USA where he formed the New York City Ballet. A great cat lover, he taught his ginger-and-white tom Mourka to do ballet movements such as *jetés* and *tours en l'air*.

Lucille Ball (1911–89)

US actress. The popular red-haired comedienne who was best known for her long-running TV series, *I Love Lucy* (1951–55), *The Lucy Show* (1962–68) and *Here's Lucy* (1968–73) had a mongrel dog called Junior and a number of cats.

Tallulah Bankhead (1903–68)

US actress. Famous for her stage roles in *The Little Foxes* (1939), written by LILLIAN HELLMAN, and *The Skin of Our Teeth* (1942), Tallulah Bankhead also played a memorable part in the film *Lifeboat* (1944). She had a cat named Dolly and also owned a pet lion cub which she named after Winston Churchill. When the lion got too big she gave it to the Bronx Zoo in New York. In addition she kept birds: 'I have a bird that says who are you? and laughs just like me and Gaylord the parakeet who drinks champagne.'

Sarah Bernhardt (1844–1923)

French-born actress. The founder of her own theatre in 1899, the Théâtre Sarah Bernhardt (in which she regularly played Hamlet), this famous one-legged actress also had a dog called Hamlet.

In her autobiography, *My Double Life* (1907), she describes her three dogs, Minniccio, Bull and Fly, her parrot Bizibouzou and her monkey Darwin when living at 77 Chester Square, London. She also recalls her visit to Cross's Zoo in Liverpool in search of a pair of lions but instead she bought a cheetah ('It was quite young and very droll; it looked like a gargoyle on some castle in the Middle Ages') and 'a dog-wolf, all white with a thick coat, fiery eyes and spear-like teeth'. In addition she was given six small chameleons and a magnificent large one:

> a prehistoric, fabulous sort of animal. It was a veritable Chinese curiosity, and changed colour from pale green to dark bronze, at one minute slender and long like a lily leaf, and then all at once puffed out and thick-set like a toad [...] I was delighted and quite enthusiastic over this present. I named my chameleon 'Cross-çi, Cross-ça' in honour of Mr Cross.

However, her servants were not quite so keen on the animals, particularly the dog-wolf, and when the cheetah was let out of its cage in the garden in London bedlam ensued to the terror of everyone except Bernhardt, who thought it was all most amusing.

When living in the Boulevard Péreire in Paris in the 1890s she had a gilded cage in which were kept tiger-cubs. Wherever she went Bernhardt brought back animals. After a tour of Australia these included 'my St Bernard, "Auckland", the opossums, the "native bear" [a koala?], and others, but few long survived the change of climate'.

Alexander Borodin (1833–87)

Russian composer. Borodin's works include the unfin-
ished opera *Prince Igor* and three symphonies. He owned
a number of tomcats, including Rybolov and Dlinyenki.
The Borodin family's menagerie was later described by
fellow composer Rimsky-Korsakov:

> Several tom-cats that found a home in Borodin's apartment
> paraded across the dinner-table, sticking their noses into
> plates, unceremoniously leaping to the diners' backs ... One
> tabby was called Rybolov ('Fisherman'), because, in the win-
> ter, he contrived to catch small fish with his paw through the
> ice-holes; the other was called Dlinyenki ('Longy') and he was
> in the habit of fetching homeless kittens by the neck to
> Borodin's apartment ... Then there were other, and less
> remarkable specimens of the genus felis. You might sit at
> their tea-table, – and behold! Tommy marches along the
> board and makes for your plate ... Meantime, zip! another cat
> has bounded at Alyeksandr Porfiryevich's neck and, twining
> himself about it, has fallen to warming that neck without
> pity. 'Listen, dear Sir, this is too much of a good thing!' says
> Borodin, but without stirring; and the cat lolls blissfully on.

Johannes Brahms (1833–97)

German composer. Brahms' best-known work is *The
German Requiem* but he also wrote more than 200 songs
and a number of piano sonatas among other composi-
tions. Brahms reputedly hated cats and used to shoot
arrows at them. Yet curiously he was very fond of the
works of E.T.A. Hoffman , especially *Kater Murr* (The Cat

Murr), and when composing lighter works even used the pseudonym 'Johannes Kreisler Junior' (Kreisler being the fictional musician who owned the cat Murr).

Benjamin Britten (1913–76)

British composer. Perhaps best known for his operas *Peter Grimes* (1945) and *Billy Budd* (1951), Britten had a long relationship with the singer Peter Pears. When living in Aldeburgh, Suffolk, he owned a female dachshund called Clytie (named after Pears's American singing teacher Clytie Mundy), which was photographed by Karsh in 1954.

Charlie Chaplin (1889–1977)

British-born actor and film director. The great movie comedian who arrived in Hollywood in 1914 where he starred in such films as *The Gold Rush*, *City Lights*, *Modern Times* and *The Great Dictator*, was also very fond of animals of all types. One day, when living in Hollywood, a skunk found its way into one of the family's bathrooms, rolled itself up on the bathmat and went to sleep. It quickly became a favourite with the Chaplins and remained with them for several weeks. According to the actor James Mason, who was a neighbour and a friend of the family, 'Chaplin was intrigued by the way it used its hands. It could open any one of the kitchen closets on which the doorknobs were sufficiently close to the ground.' However, as Mason also recorded, the skunk's departure was as sudden as was its arrival. One day the Chaplins decided that if the skunk was going to be accepted as a permanent member of the household it would have to be 'altered'. In consequence they sent for a vet and the necessary operation was duly performed. However, perhaps not surprisingly, the skunk saw this as an unfriendly gesture and promptly returned to the woods.

Chaplin also owned cats and in 1947 two of their kittens went missing. As their nearest Hollywood neighbour was the actor Glenn Ford – who had a large dog – it was at first suspected that his mutt was the culprit. However, having thoroughly investigated the case and thereby proved the dog's innocence, they decided that the kittens must have been killed by coyotes.

Anton Chekhov (1860–1904)

Russian playwright and short-story writer. Best known as the author of such plays as *Uncle Vanya* (1900) and *The Cherry Orchard* (1904), when living in Yalta, Chekhov had two pet mongrel dogs and a crane.

Fryderyk Chopin (1810–49)

Polish composer and pianist. Chopin's fame rests on his many piano works which include the celebrated funeral march as well as preludes, nocturnes, waltzes, mazurkas, polonaises, three sonatas and two concertos. His first published work appeared when he was still at school and it is assumed that he owned a cat as Waltz No. 3 in F major was inspired by a cat walking over the keys (see also DOMENICO SCARLATTI). From 1838 to 1847 Chopin lived in France with the novelist George Sand (1804–76, whose real name was Aurore, Baroness Dudevant, a relative of the King of Poland) and they kept a stray dog called Mops (Polish for pug-dog). Chopin also enjoyed riding horses.

James Dean (1931–55)

US actor. Dean became an overnight success in *East of Eden* (1955) and only made two more films – *Rebel Without a Cause* (1955) and *Giant* (1956) – before being killed in a car crash. His celebrity career lasted just over a year. Dean had a cat called Marcus which was a gift from Elizabeth Taylor who starred with him in *Giant.*

Claude Debussy (1862–1918)

French composer. Debussy's famous works include *The Sea* (1905) and *Prelude à l'après-midi d'un faune* (1894, based on the poem by STÉPHANE MALLARMÉ). He was also very fond of cats and owned a succession of grey angoras all named Line.

Sir Edward Elgar (1857–1934)

British composer. In Elgar's famous *Enigma Variations* (1899) series, 'Variation XI (G.R.S.)' represent Dan who was a bulldog owned by his friend George Robertson Sinclair, organist of Hereford Cathedral. Elgar said that while out walking with Sinclair and the dog, Dan fell down a bank of the River Wye and into the river. He then paddled upstream to find a landing place and, on arriving there safely, barked. Sinclair asked Elgar to set the event to music and he did.

After the death of his wife Elgar had a spaniel called Mario and a Cairn terrier called Mina.

Clark Gable (1901–06)

US actor. The 'King of Hollywood' was perhaps best known for playing the part of Rhett Butler in the hugely successful film *Gone With the Wind* (1939) based on the book by MARGARET MITCHELL and also starring VIVEN LEIGH. Gable and his third wife, actress Carol Lombard (1908–42), had a dachshund called Commissioner.

W.S. Gilbert (1836–1911)

British librettist. William Schwenk Gilbert, who wrote the verses for the famous Gilbert & Sullivan comic operas (the musical scores were by SIR ARTHUR SULLIVAN), was a keen animal lover. At his home, Graeme's Dyke in Harrow Weald, not far from Windsor Castle, he kept Jersey cows, horses, chickens, pigs, bees and pigeons (for whom he built an ornate pigeon-house). In the entrance hall to his house he kept a parrot in a cage which was considered to be the finest talker in England and which could whistle a hornpipe. He also sometimes took in less gifted parrots. Interviewed in 1891 he pointed to another such bird in the hallway: 'The other parrot, who is a novice, belongs to Dr Playfair. He is reading up with my bird, who takes pupils.'

Van Heflin (1910–71)

US actor. Born Emmett Evan Heflin Jr, the son of a French-Irish dentist, Van Heflin worked in the theatre before coming to Hollywood and won an Oscar for *Johnny Eager* in 1941. He married the actress Frances Neal in 1942 (divorced 1967). In their happier days Van Heflin and his wife owned a number of cats, two of which appear in the memoirs of fellow actor, friend and Hollywood neighbour, James Mason. These were named Mousetrap and Silkhat, and they had a habit of eating lizards during the summer months. In consequence they would become very thin as a result of the poison that the lizards contained. However, when the autumn came they returned to their normal size. As Mason recorded: 'Come the fall the Heflin cats inflate to the dimensions favoured by overfed domestic shorthairs, lizard being no longer in season.'

Lillian Hellman (1905–84)

US playwright. Best known for such works as *The Little Foxes* (1939), which was later made into a film starring Bette Davis, Hellman's long-time companion was the detective writer Dashiell Hammett. After he died she lived in Vineyard Haven on the island of Martha's Vineyard, Massachusetts, and kept a large poodle with a loud bark to discourage visitors.

Audrey Hepburn (1929–93)

Belgian-born actress. It was after being noticed by the French writer COLETTE – who chose her to star in the Broadway production of her novel *Gigi* (1951) – that Hepburn's career took off and she won an Oscar for *Roman Holiday* (1953). Other celebrated films in which she starred include *Breakfast at Tiffany's*, based on the novel of the same name by TRUMAN CAPOTE, and *My Fair Lady* which won eight Oscars and was based on the play *Pygmalion* by GEORGE BERNARD SHAW. Hepburn owned a Yorkshire terrier called Mr Famous.

Henrik Ibsen (1828–1906)

Norwegian playwright. Ibsen first came to fame with his plays *Brand* and *Peer Gynt* and later produced such masterpieces as *Ghosts*, *Hedda Gabler* and *A Doll's House*. While writing *Brand* (1866) he kept a pet scorpion in a beer-glass on his desk.

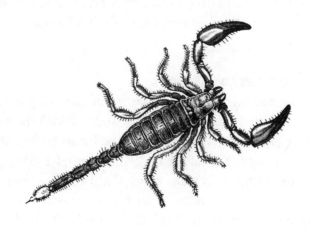

Sir Henry Irving (1838–1905)

British actor and theatre manager. Born John Henry Brodribb, Irving was the greatest English actor of his time and in 1878 began a theatrical relationship with ELLEN TERRY at London's Lyceum Theatre which lasted until 1902. He was also the first actor to receive a knighthood. When interviewed in his house in Grafton Street near Bond Street, London, in 1892 he had a small black-and-white (largely white) male terrier called Fussie who had originally been owned by the champion jockey Fred Archer. Archer gave the puppy to Ellen Terry when she was visiting Newmarket stables and she subsequently gave him to Irving. For his birthday in 1889 Terry gave Irving a photo of the dog sitting on her lap with another dog Ned. The inscription ran: 'We wish you many happy returns of the day, and shall ever remain your loving, faithful friends, Fussie and Ned, Feb. 6, 1889.' The dog used to go to the theatre every night with its master and would patiently sit on a mat in his dressing-room until the performance was over. When Fussie died he was buried in the dogs' cemetery in Hyde Park, London.

Vivien Leigh (1913–67)

British actress. Born Vivien Hartley in Darjeeling, India, and educated at a convent school and at RADA she had overnight success with *The Mask of Virtue* (1935). She married Laurence Olivier in 1940 (divorced 1961) and starred with him in many classical plays such as *Romeo and Juliet.* She won an Oscar for her performance as Scarlett O'Hara in the 1939 film *Gone With the Wind.*

Leigh owned a number of cats including Poo Jones, Nichols and Boy (a Sealpoint Siamese).

Maurice Maeterlinck (1862–1949)

Belgian dramatist, poet and essayist. Best known for his prose-play *Pelléas et Mélisande* (1892), on which CLAUDE DEBUSSY based his opera, Maeterlinck won the Nobel Prize for Literature in 1911. He was also very fond of dogs and owned a small, black French bulldog called Pelléas. When he died he wrote an essay on him, 'On the Death of a Little Dog'. He also featured in *Pelléas et Mélisande* where he is described as having

> a great, bulging, powerful forehead, like that of Socrates or Verlaine; and under a little black nose, blunt as a churlish assent, a pair of large, hanging and symmetrical chops, which made his head a sort of massive, obstinate, pensive and three-cornered menace.

Jayne Mansfield (1933–67)

US actress. Born Vera Jayne Palmer, Jayne Mansfield is best known for her parts in films such as *The Female Jungle* (1955) and *The Girl Can't Help It* (1956). She owned a small female dog which was killed with her and two others when her Buick Electra car was involved in a crash in Louisiana.

James Mason (1909–84)

British actor. Born in Huddersfield, Yorkshire, Mason originally studied architecture but later became a distinguished screen and theatre actor and was three times nominated for Oscars. As a child of 12 in Huddersfield he was given a Manchester terrier by the headmaster of his boarding school, 'a sad black and tan bitch called Nell'. The dog was very thin, with an inclination to bow-leggedness, and had big, down-hanging ears, a longish rat-like tail, a sharp muzzle, and tan feet 'with little black pencil marks on the toes.'

Mason was also a great cat lover and even wrote and illustrated a book about them, *The Cats in Our Lives* (1949). Among his pets were Whitey and Folly and a stray called Lady Leeds which he found in the railway station in Leeds. Others included the Siamese cats Sadie, Topboy, Tree and Flower-Face. In fact it was a Siamese cat that introduced him to his wife. They met at a party in 1935 and in the course of conversation his future wife described her cat Gemma to him. Mason said that he had never actually been in close proximity to a Siamese before, though he had admired them from a distance. In consequence she invited him to her home to meet Gemma and their romance blossomed.

Marilyn Monroe (1926–62)

US actress. Born Norma Jean Mortenson, Monroe made her name with films such as *Gentlemen Prefer Blondes*, *Some Like it Hot* and *The Prince and the Showgirl*. She had a poodle called Mafia which was a gift from Frank

Sinatra and a Bassett hound with white paws called Hugo while she was married to her third husband, playwright Arthur Miller. She also had a white Persian cat called Mitsou.

Wolfgang Amadeus Mozart (1756–91)
Austrian composer. Mozart is alleged to have owned a pet starling which he taught to whistle the theme of the last movement of his G Major Piano Concerto (K453).

Dame Anna Neagle (1904–86)
British actress. Born Marjorie Robertson, Anna Neagle married the director Herbert Wilcox and became a major star of historical films dramas such as *The Lady with the Lamp* (1951). She also had a cat called Tuppence.

Eugene O'Neill (1888–1953)
US dramatist. Awarded the Nobel Prize for Literature in 1936 – the first US dramatist to receive the honour – O'Neill is perhaps best known for his masterpiece, *Long Day's Journey into Night*, which was published after his death, in 1956. O'Neill owned a Dalmatian called Blemie which he bought when he was living in France in 1929–31 with his third wife, Carlotta. The couple doted on the dog like a child and even bought it a coat made by Hermès. Its full name was Silverdeen Emblem O'Neill and when it was near death in 1940, O'Neill wrote an essay on it entitled 'The Last Will and Testament of Silverdeen Emblem O'Neill'.

Max Ophuls (1902–57)

German-born film director. Born Max Oppenheimer in Saarbrücken, Germany, Ophuls took French nationality in the plebiscite of 1934 and directed films in Germany, France and the USA before returning to France where he had his greatest successes with *La Ronde* (1950) and *Lola Montez* (1955). According to the actor James Mason, who starred in Ophuls' films *Caught* and *The Reckless Moment* (both 1949) he had a number of cats including 'a remarkably beautiful white Persian'.

Larry Parks (1914–75)

US actor. The star of the Oscar-winning film *The Jolson Story* (1946) – itself about the star of the first motion picture with sound, *The Jazz Singer* (1927) – Parks and his wife Betty Garrett had a blue cream Persian cat called Pepper which was mute.

Anna Pavlova (1881–1931)

Russian-born ballerina. Born in St Petersburg, Pavolova rose to fame with her portrayal of 'The Dying Swan'. As a memento of this role an admirer gave her a pair of mute swans, the male of which she named Jack. The two swans lived on the lake at her London home, Ivy House, Golders Green, and Jack would wrap his long neck around Pavlova's. She also owned a Boston terrier and a French bulldog.

Sir Arthur Pinero (1855–1934)

British playwright. A member of SIR HENRY IRVING's Lyceum Company, Pinero was the most successful dramatist of his day and was perhaps best known for his play *The Second Mrs Tanqueray* (1893). He owned a collie dog called Collie Cibber (named after the eighteenth-century actor, playwright and Poet Laureate).

Beryl Reid (1920–96)

British comedienne and actress. Beryl Reid was born in Hereford and her first starring role was as the schoolgirl Monica in the BBC radio comedy series *Educating Archie*. She received a Tony award for the Broadway production of *The Killing of Sister George* in 1966 (first performed in London starring HERMIONE BADDELEY) and later acted the same role in the 1968 film of the play. Reid also owned a number of cats and in her book *A Passion for Cats* she described how one of her wartime companions helped save her life. During the London Blitz, the cat would hide whenever a German plane went overhead but would ignore any British planes, thus giving Reid time to take cover before the bombs began to drop.

Other cats she owned included Cleopatra, Fred and Jenny. At the time of writing her autobiography *So Much Love* (1984), she owned 10 cats: Billy, Clive, Elsie (a tortoiseshell), Dimly, Sir Harry (an enormous tabby named after SIR HARRY SECOMBE), Muriel (a long-haired Old English tortoiseshell), Ronnie, Emma (who had lost one eye) and Georgie Girl (then 20 years old). The tenth was a cat of independent mind called Lulu, 'who one day decided she wanted to live outside the house. I went up the ladder to feed her four times a day on the roof, which people around used to think was a bit eccentric.' Curiously, none of her cats ever liked fish.

Sir Ralph Richardson (1902–83)

British actor. Famed for his theatre work as much as his films, Richardson had major roles in the movies *Anna Karenina* (1948), *Oh! What a Lovely War* (1969) and *A Doll's House* (1973) among others. When living in Chester Terrace, London, he also owned a green parrot with clipped wings called José which he kept on an open perch rather than in a cage. To give it a change of air, and much to the amusement of onlookers, every morning he would drive his motorcycle around the Outer Circle of Regents Park, with José perched on his shoulder! He had bought the parrot in Spain while filming *Dr Zhivago* and smuggled it back to Britain by doping it with brandy and then hiding it away in an inside pocket of his jacket. Unfortunately, however, it awoke midway through the flight to London and caused chaos among the passengers on the plane until he managed to get some more brandy from the stewardess and put it back to sleep again.

Richardson also owned ferrets and a hamster.

Roy Rogers (1912–98)

US actor. Roy Rogers, whose real name was Leonard Franklin Slye, was celebrated for his screen appearances with his horse Trigger. Trigger was a gold palomino with a white mane and tail which Rogers originally bought for $2500 in 1938. He featured in more than 100 films with Rogers and also appeared on television in the 1950s. Rogers even made a film tribute to the horse, *My Pal Trigger*, in 1946. As well as Trigger, Rogers owned a German Shepherd dog called Bullet who also featured in films such as *Spoilers of the Plains* (1951). Both Trigger and Bullet were stuffed when they died and put on display in the Roy Rogers-Dale Evans Museum in Victorville, California.

Domenico Scarlatti (1685–1757)
Italian composer. Scarlatti wrote more than 500 sonatas for the harpsichord and composed several operas for the Queen of Poland. His famous *Cat Fugue* was supposedly inspired by the sounds produced when his pet cat Pulcinella walked over the keys of his harpsichord.

Sir Harry Secombe (1921–2001)
British comedian. The famous member of *The Goon Show* had a boxer dog called Jim. A somewhat rotund figure, his friend BERYL REID named one of her cats, Sir Harry – a huge ginger tabby tom – in his honour.

Mack Sennett (1880–1960)
US film director. The celebrated US film director who created the Keystone Kops comedy film series and directed many others (including some starring CHARLIE

CHAPLIN) was also the first director to put a cat in his films. This was a grey stray which appeared on the set one day while Sennett was filming and he immediately made it part of the scene. Sennett named her Pepper and she later starred in other films – the only cat ever to appear in silent movies. The Sennett studio also had a Great Dane dog called Teddy.

George Bernard Shaw (1856–1950)

Irish dramatist. Shaw was awarded the Nobel Prize for Literature in 1935 and is best known for such works as *Arms and the Man*, *The Devil's Disciple*, *Man and Superman*, *Major Barbara* and *Pygmalion*. He was not a great animal lover but once briefly owned a canary, 'a little green brute', that had flown in through an open window one day. However, they did not get on well – 'I hated it and it hated me' – and he was greatly relieved when one day somebody stole it. Thus he was far from pleased when he received another bird as a gift from his friend Francis Collison in 1903. Shaw wrote back indignantly, asking him what on earth had possessed him to send it, saying that: 'I am a vegetarian, and can't eat it; and it is not big enough to eat me.' In desperation he eventually decided to give the canary to his gardener's wife with the offer of the cage and 'five shillings a week for the term of it natural life. I shall then hear it only when I walk in the garden; and at every trill I shall curse the name of F. Collison.'

Dame Ethyl Smyth (1858–1944)

British composer. As well as composing such operas as *The Wreckers* (1906) Ethyl Smyth was a keen suffragette and wrote 'The March of the Women' in 1911. She kept Old English sheepdogs and a St Bernard called Marco.

Dusty Springfield (1939–99)

British singer. Born Mary O'Brien, Dusty Springfield originally appeared as part of the folk/country trio The Springfields but had a huge hit with her first solo song 'I Only Want to be With You' in 1964. Towards the end of her life she had two cats. One these, Nicholas Alexis, was named after the haemophiliac son of the last Russian Tsar (NICHOLAS II) because he was always ill. The other, Malaysia, was run over by a car in England just after Springfield had finished recording her album *Reputation* (1990). As a result she dedicated the album to the cat.

August Strindberg (1849–1912)

Swedish playwright and novelist. Best known for such plays as *The Father* and *Miss Julie*, Strindberg evidently was not fond of dogs as he once wrote: 'I loathe people who keep dogs. They are cowards who haven't got the guts to bite people themselves.'

Sir Arthur Sullivan (1842–1900)

British composer. Sir Arthur Sullivan is best known for his collaboration with W.S. GILBERT in the Gilbert & Sullivan comic operas. In 1897, when living in Walton-on-Thames, Surrey, he owned an elderly female parrot called Polly that used to repeat 'Polly! What's the time?' at regular intervals.

Dame Ellen Terry (1847–1928)

British actress. The leading Shakespearean actress of her day, Ellen Terry – in partnership with SIR HENRY IRVING – dominated the English and US theatre scene from 1878 to 1902. She owned a number of pets and when interviewed at her home, Tower Cottage, in Winchelsea,

Sussex, in 1892 had a pony called Tommy and a terrier dog called Punch. Punch was not very well trained and she had difficulty getting him to lie down or 'die': 'Dead! Dead, sir! dead little doggy. Why won't you die? I really think this dog is as mad as a hatter. If he doesn't alter, I shall certainly call him "The Hatter". Die doggy, die!' She also kept a bullfinch called Prince in an ornate brass-wire cage in her drawing-room overlooking the garden. Of him she said:

> He pipes all day and we don't quite know what the tune is. When I bought him he was in a little wooden cage and on it were written in pencil the names of two songs – 'Du Bist Wie Eine Blume' and – what do you think? – 'Poli Berkins'! But he's never whistled 'My Pretty Polly Perkins of Paddington Green' to this day.

She also owned a cat called Minnie which she rescued as a stray.

> At a pretty roadside inn we found a wee kitten – it seemed to like me. It came running out to us and appeared lost. It gave such a funny little whine, which seemed to say 'Me-e-ne-e', so I christened it Minnie on the spot.

In addition she owned a tortoise.

A fox-terrier called Fussie was given her by the champion jockey Fred Archer and she subsequently gave him to SIR HENRY IRVING. Other fox-terriers she owned included Bossy and Drummy, and she also had a least two other dogs, Winkie and Charley.

Sir Herbert Beerbohm Tree (1853–1917)

British actor-manager. The half-brother of MAX BEER-BOHM, Tree took over the Haymarket Theatre in London in 1887 and built Her Majesty's Theatre opposite it in 1897 where his productions rivalled those of SIR HENRY IRVING at the Lyceum in the Strand. He founded the Royal Academy of Dramatic Art in 1904. One of his great successes was the first ever production of *Pygmalion* (1914) by GEORGE BERNARD SHAW. When living in an old house on Hampstead Heath he owned a cow, and a photo of his daughter Viola taken in 1897 shows her with a large mongrel dog.

Rudolph Valentino (1895–1926)

Italian-born actor. Born in Castellaneta, Italy, Valentino's real name was Rodolpho Alfonzo Raffaello Pierre Gilibert Gugliemi di Valentina d'Antongulla. He originally studied agriculture before emigrating to the USA in 1913 and first appeared on stage as a dancer. He was made a star by the film *The Four Horsemen of the Apocalypse* (1921) and became the 'screen lover' for which he is best known in the four films *The Sheikh* (1921), *Blood and Sand* (1922), *The Eagle* (1925) and *The Son of the Sheikh* (1926), but never worked in sound films. He died of a perforated ulcer (peritonitis) in New York at the age of 31 – 100,000 telegrams were sent on news of his death and the crowd of mourners stretched for 11 blocks. Valentino owned a German Shepherd dog called Prince and a Doberman called Kabar which is buried in the Pet Memorial Cemetery in Calabasas, California.

Ralph Vaughan Williams (1872–1958)

British composer. As well as writing nine symphonies and an opera, Vaughan Williams was a keen animal lover and showed his appreciation for birds in his celebrated delicate violin piece 'The Lark Ascending'. When he moved to London in 1953 he owned two kittens, Crispin and Friskin.

Richard Wagner (1813–83)

German composer. Wagner is best known for his *Ring* cycle of operas as well as *Tristan und Isolde* and *Die Meistersinger*. He later said that the idea for *Der Fliegende Holländer* came to him while fleeing creditors and in a sense was a direct result of his love for his Newfoundland dog called Robber. The story has it that in July 1839 he and his wife Minna, together with Robber, illegally crossed the Prussian-Russian border at night and because Minna would not have the dog in the carriage (she made him trot behind for the first day and he later had to lie on the roof) they eventually ended up travelling by boat to Copenhagen and thence in rough seas to England. It was this sea voyage that inspired the piece.

Wagner later owned a dog called Peps and a parrot called Papo.

John Wayne (1907–79)

US actor. Born Marion Michael Morrison, John Wayne first came to fame as the Ringo Kid in *Stagecoach* (1939). In all he made more than 80 films and won an Oscar for *True Grit* in 1969. As a child he had a pet called Duke – an Airedale dog – which was the source of the actor's nickname.

Belles-
Lettres

J.R. Ackerley (1896–1967)

British journalist and author. For many years (1935-59) literary editor of the *The Listener* magazine, J.R.Ackerley is perhaps best known for his book *My Dog Tulip* (1956), which was based on his own female Alsatian Queenie. (His 1960 novel *We Think the World of You* is also based on the dog.) In *My Dog Tulip* Ackerley described how the dog accidentally bit him once when she mistook his hand for a rotten apple they were both trying to grab simultaneously. When the dog saw the bandage on his hand she was very upset and crept away to 'the darkest corner of the bedroom, and stayed there for the rest of the afternoon'.

Sir Max Beerbohm (1872–1956)

British critic, essayist and caricaturist. Max Beerbohm, who signed his famous caricatures simply 'Max' and was known as 'The Incomparable Max' is also well-known as the author of the novel *Zuleika Dobson* (1911). When living in Villino Chiaro in Italy, Beerbohm had a number of pets named after literary figures. A fox-terrier acquired in 1913 was named James after HENRY JAMES – whose work Beerbohm admired and who had then just celebrated his 70th birthday – but pronounced Yah-mès so that the locals could say its name. In 1920 he was given a kitten which he named Strechi, after LYTTON STRACHEY. Two years later he wrote to the author of *Eminent Victorians* about the cat:

The kitten of whom I told you last year is now a confirmed cat. He is much larger than he seemed likely to become, and is vigorous and vagrant, but not, I am sorry to say, either affectionate or intelligent. It is not known that he ever caught a mouse; he dislikes rain, but has no knowledge of how to avoid it if it falls; and if one caresses him he is very likely to scratch one. He is, however, very proud of his name, and sends his respectful regards to his Illustrissimo Eponymisto Inglese.

Thomas Carlyle (1795–1881)

Scottish essayist and historian. Perhaps best known for his *History of the French Revolution* (1837) Carlyle was not fond of animals though he did own a horse called Larry. However, his wife Jane received a small white mongrel terrier called Nero from a friend in 1849, of which she was very fond and which her husband came to like and took for walks over the next ten years. He once jumped from a window in the Carlyles' house in Chelsea, an incident which is mentioned in *Flush* (1933), a spoof biography by VIRGINIA WOOLF of the spaniel owned by ELIZABETH BARRETT BROWNING.

The Carlyles also had a black cat called Columbine and a canary (described by Carlyle with disgust as 'the most inanely chimerical of all') which both feature in a letter from Jane Carlyle to a friend. At great expense Mrs Carlyle had had the canary's cage attached by a chain and pulley to the drawing-room ceiling to escape the interest of the cat which spent 'all its spare time in gazing up at the bird with eyes aflame!' Thinking the bird was now safe, she went out for a walk only to discover on her return that the cat had leapt up from a table, pulled down the cage and smashed up valuable ornaments.

> You never saw such a scene of devastation. The carpet was covered with fragments of a pretty terracotta basket given me by Lady Airlie – and fragments of the glass which covered it, and with the earth and ferns that had been growing in it and with birdseed, and bits of brass chain, and I can't tell what all! That is what one gets by breeding up a cat! – She had rushed right out by the back door and didn't show her face for twenty-four hours after! And now I don't know where the poor bird will be safe.

Giacomo Casanova (1725–98)

Italian adventurer and writer. Despite the reputation he gathered as a libertine and philanderer, Casanova was well educated, wrote more than 20 books, moved among high society and was presented at court to FREDERICK THE GREAT of Prussia, CATHERINE THE GREAT of Russia and GEORGE III of England. Among other pets, Casanova owned a female fox-terrier called Melampyge, about which he wrote verses when she died, and another called Finette.

Having made a small fortune on a lottery he had set up in Paris, Casanova arrived in London at the age of 37, took a house in Pall Mall and, not being able to speak English himself, employed a Negro manservant who spoke English, French and Italian. In September 1763 he came across a very attractive young Swiss woman whom he had met in the Bazaar in Paris as a girl of 13 and to whom he had then given some shoe buckles. Now going by the name of Charpillon and living with her mother and aunts in London, she became the instrument of Casanova's downfall. After teasing Casanova to distraction by offering her favours and then withdrawing them – he had even rented her a house in  Chelsea – she had him arrested on the grounds of intending to do her grievous bodily harm and he was brought up before the famous blind magistrate, Sir John Fielding, half-brother of the novelist Henry Fielding. Facing a potential life-sentence in Newgate, Casanova nonetheless managed to gain his release and vowed to get his vengeance on the Charpillon woman and her family. To this end he happened to be walking about the parrot market which then existed in London when he spotted a particularly fine specimen in a cage and an idea started to form in his mind. He asked the people selling the bird what language it spoke:

> They told me it was quite young and did not speak at all yet,
> so I bought it for ten guineas. I thought I would teach the bird
> a pretty speech, so I had the cage hung by my bed, and

repeated dozens of times every day the following sentence: 'The Charpillon is a bigger wh**re than her mother.' [...] In a fortnight the bird had learnt the phrase with the utmost exactness; and every time it uttered the words it accompanied them with a shriek of laughter which I had not taught it, but which made me laugh myself.

He then gave the bird to his manservant to take to the Exchange to sell. A couple of days passed without a buyer as the parrot only spoke French, but once word got about among high society – for the girl had teased other noblemen before Casanova, such as Lord Pembroke – there were many bidders and the Charpillon and her mother were furious when they heard about it. However, as a parrot cannot be indicted for libel, they were helpless. In fact so successful was Casanova's ploy that an article even appeared about the parrot in the *St James's Chronicle* before it was eventually sold to Lord Grosvenor, who himself had designs on the young woman and hoped to gain her favours by silencing the slanderous bird.

Vicomte de Chateaubriand (1768–1848)

French writer and diplomat. One of the major figures of the French Romantic movement – whose famous autobiography was not published as a whole until 1902 – Chateaubriand later became French Ambassador to London. When working briefly as French Ambassador in Rome he also inherited Micetto, the famous cat of POPE LEO XII, when the pope died in 1829. Chateaubriand later described the cat:

I have as a companion a fat red-grey cat with black cross stripes, born at the Vatican in the Raphael Gallery: Leo XII brought it up in the skirt of his robe, where I used to watch it with envy, when the Pontiff gave me my audience as Ambassador. On the death of the successor of St Peter, I inherited the cat without a master [...]. They called it Micetto, surnamed the Pope's Cat. In this capacity it enjoys an extreme consideration among pious souls. I strive to make it forget exile, the Sistine Chapel and the sun of Michael Angelo's dome, on which it used to take its walks far removed from earth.

Chateaubriand later also wrote:

I value in the cat the independent and almost ungrateful spirit which prevents her from attaching herself to anyone, the indifference with which she passes from the salon to the housetop. When we caress her, she stretches herself and arches her back responsively; but this is because she feels an agreeable sensation, not because she takes a silly satisfaction, like the dog, in faithfully loving a thankless master. The cat lives alone, has no need of society, obeys only when she pleases, pretends to sleep that she may see the more clearly and scratches everything on which she can lay her paw.

John Evelyn (1620–1706)

British diarist. A contemporary of CHARLES II, John Evelyn commented in his famous diaries on the foul state of the king's palace as a result of his addiction to spaniels. Evelyn himself owned a black horse and while in Rome had a spaniel which was later stolen.

Anne Frank (1929–45)

German-Jewish diarist. While hiding from the Nazis in a house in Amsterdam for two years (1942-44) Anne Frank had a tomcat called Mouschi. On one occasion the cat, having no dry earth in its box, peed onto some wood-shavings on the floor in the loft above their room. Before long this dripped down onto the family below and onto a barrel of potatoes. Pandemonium ensued which caused Anne no end of merriment as the poor cat crouched under a chair while everyone dashed about the room with bleach and floorcloths. The woodshavings and pota-toes stank of cat pee and her father had to gather them all up together into a bucket to be burned. As Anne recorded in her diary that day: 'Poor Mouschi! How were you to know that peat is unobtainable?'

Sir Edmund Gosse (1849–1928)

British writer and critic. Gosse is best known both for his critical works and his autobiography, *Father and Son* (1907). When living at Hanover Terrace, London, he owned a black cat with green eyes called Caruso. After he died Gosse acquired another called Buchanan. Though devoted to Caruso, Gosse described him in a letter to the poet JOHN DRINKWATER in 1915 as being possessed of a 'fierce contempt and sneering malice' and said that he was 'without any question the most ungenerous cat in Christendom. There is no doubt that he is a German at heart, and he rules us on the system of "frightfulness". There is a theory that the atrocious soul of Nietzsche has entered into him.'

Horace Greeley (1811–72)

US journalist. Greeley founded the *New York Tribune* in 1841 and in it famously proclaimed 'Go West, Young Man' but stayed east himself, in New York's Gramercy Park district where he kept goats in his garden.

Thomas Hood (1799–1845)

British journalist and writer. In his old age Hood owned a large and very handsome dog of uncertain breed called Dash which was also very unruly and he eventually gave it away to CHARLES LAMB. Hood also owned a number of cats and wrote a poem about them which begins:

> Our old cat has kittens three –
> What do you think their names should be?
> Pepperpot, Sootikin, Scratchway-there,
> Was there ever a kitten with these to compare?
> And we call their old mother – now what do you think?
> Tabitha Long-claws Tiddley-wink!

Pepperpot was a tabby with emerald eyes, Sootikin was black with a white frill and white feet and Scratchaway was a tortoiseshell.

Jerome K. Jerome (1859–1927)

British writer. Jerome K. Jerome once owned a cat whose 'brains had run entirely to motherliness' and who brought up an orphaned spaniel puppy and a squirrel as her own. The cat would box the poor dog's ears every time it barked and no matter how many times she held down the squirrel's bushy tail with her paws and licked it to make it stay flat like a normal cat's tail, it just flicked back over the squirrel's head again.

Jerome also had a kitten called Tittums, a fox-terrier called Tim and another dog called Gustavus Adolphus, all of whom are described in *Idle Thoughts of an Idle Fellow* (1889). On one occasion Gustavus Adophus disturbed Jerome's work by barking on the stairs and he went to see what was the matter:

> It was Tittums. She was sitting on the top stair but one, and wouldn't let him pass.
>
> Tittums is our kitten. She is about the size of a penny roll. Her back was up, and she was swearing like a medical student.
>
> She does swear fearfully. [...] I told her she ought to be ashamed of herself, brought up in a Christian family as she was, too. I don't mind hearing an old cat swear, but I can't bear to see a mere kitten give way to it. It seems sad in one so young.
>
> I put Tittums in my pocket, and returned to my desk. I forgot her for the moment, and when I looked I found that she had squirmed out of my pocket on to the table, and was trying to swallow the pencil; then she put her leg into the ink-pot and upset it; then she licked her leg; then she swore again – at me this time.
>
> I put her down on the floor, and then Tim began rowing with her. I do wish Tim would mind his own business. It was no concern of his what she had been doing. Besides, he is not a saint himself. He is only a two-year-old fox terrier, and he

interferes with everything, and gives himself the airs of a grey-headed Scotch collie.

Tittums' mother has come in, and Tim has got his nose scratched, for which I am remarkably glad. I have put them all three out in the passage, where they are fighting at the present moment. I'm in a mess with the ink, and in a thundering bad temper; and if anything more in the cat or dog line comes fooling about me this morning, it had better bring its own funeral contractor with it.

The small fox-terrier dog Montmorency which features in his famous book about the adventures of three young men on a rowing holiday on the Thames, *Three Men in a Boat* (1889) – which was originally entitled *Three Men in a Boat – to Say Nothing of the Dog* – is entirely fictional, although the three men were based on real people.

Dr Samuel Johnson (1709–84)

British critic, lexicographer and poet. Dr Johnson owned a number cats over the years but the most famous of these was Hodge who is described in Boswell's *The Life of Samuel Johnson* (1791) and who was fed on a diet of oysters which Johnson himself would buy:

I shall never forget the indulgence with which he treated Hodge, his cat; for whom he himself used to go out and buy oysters, lest the servants having that trouble should take a dislike to the poor creature. I am, unluckily, one of those who have an antipathy to a cat, so that I am uneasy when in the room with one; and I own, I frequently suffered a good deal from the presence of the same Hodge. I recollect him one day scrambling up Dr Johnson's breast, apparently with much satisfaction, while my friend, smiling and half-whistling, rubbed down his back, and pulled him by the tail; and when I observed he was a fine cat, saying, 'Why, yes, Sir, but I have had cats whom I liked better than this'; and then, as if perceiving Hodge to be out of countenance, adding, 'but he is a very fine cat, a very fine cat indeed.'

Johnson also had a 'white kitling' called Lily. A statue of Hodge now stands in Gough Square outside Dr Johnson's house.

Charles Lamb (1775–1834)

British essayist. As well as his famous *Essays of Elia* (1823–33), Lamb is celebrated for the *Tales from Shakespear* [sic] co-written with his sister Mary. When living in Islington, London, Lamb inherited a large and very handsome dog of uncertain breed called Dash from the poet THOMAS HOOD. However, he was the bane of Lamb's life as he would never let Lamb leave the house without him and once taken for a walk kept disappearing when let off the lead. The writer P.G. Patmore (1786–1855), a friend of the Lambs who lived in Fulham, described one of Dash's regular habits:

> In the Regent's Park in particular Dash had his quasi-master completely at his mercy; for the moment they got within the Ring, he used to squeeze himself through the railing, and disappeared for half-an-hour together in the enclosed and thick-

ly planted greensward, knowing perfectly well that Lamb did
not dare to move from the spot where he (Dash) had disappeared till he thought proper to show himself again.

Just before moving to Enfield Chase, Lamb, driven mad
by the beast, was forced to give him away to Patmore who
found that in fact the dog had just been taking advantage
of Lamb's gentle nature, 'for as soon as he found himself
in the keeping of one who knew what dog-decorum was,
he subsided into the best-bred and best-behaved of his
species'.

Edward Lear (1812–88)

British writer and artist. The painter and nonsense-
poetry writer Edward Lear was so fond of his stubby-
tailed striped tomcat Foss – star of 'How Pleasant to
Know Mr Lear' and 'The Heraldic Blazon of Foss the Cat',
and undoubtedly the inspiration for 'The Owl and the
Pussycat' – that when he moved house in 1881 he had
the new one in San Remo, Italy, built to exactly the same
specifications as before just so that the cat would feel at
home. When Foss died on 26 November 1887 he was
buried beneath a fig-tree in the garden of Lear's house,
the Villa Tennyson, in San Remo. On his tombstone,
the inscription written in Italian says that he was 31
when he died and had spent 30 years in Lear's house.
Foss also appears in the poem 'The Courtship of Yonghy-
Bonghy-Bo':

He has many friends, layman and clerical.

> Old Foss is the name of his cat.

His body is perfectly spherical,

> He weareth a runcible hat.

Lear was also well-known as a painter of birds and was employed by the Zoological Society of London and the 13th Earl of Derby (who had a private zoo near Liverpool) and even gave QUEEN VICTORIA drawing lessons. The Lear's Macaw is named after him as he was the first person to draw it.

Dorothy Parker (1893–1967)

US writer and critic. Dorothy Parker, whose maiden name was Dorothy Rothschild, was well known as a *New Yorker* journalist, author and wit and was a member of the famous Algonquin Table of New York intellectuals which also included HAROLD ROSS. She also owned a number of cats and dogs. When interviewed by *Paris Reviews* in her small New York apartment in 1957 she had a young poodle which had the run of the place and which she said made it look 'somewhat "Hogarthian"', with newspapers and half-eaten lamb chops spread about the floor. She also used to sit in her chair and throw a battered rubber doll, 'its throat torn from ear to ear' into corners of the room for the poodle to retrieve.

Parker named one of her dogs Woodrow Wilson because he was 'full of shit' and called her canary Onan (after the biblical character) because it kept spilling its seed on the ground. At one stage she also had a pet alligator.

Samuel Pepys (1633–1703)

British diarist. The last descendant of Pepys's cat was Brutus, who lived at the National Gallery until his death in 1933. Pepys also loved to hear the singing of caged canaries. In his *Diary* (8 February 1660) he records that his wife's brother had given them 'a pretty black dog which I liked well', though four days later he threatened to throw it out the window 'if he pissed the house any more' and on 19 February it gave birth to four puppies.

Harold Ross (1892–1951)

Journalist. The famous founder-editor of the *New Yorker* and prominent member of the Algonquin Table – which also included DOROTHY PARKER – had a cat called Missus which he planned to mate with a white angora cat called Miztah owned by the humorist Franklin Pierce Adams. Unfortunately Missus disappeared one night shortly before the match was made.

Sir Richard Steele (1672–1729)

British essayist and journalist. Steele was editor of the *London Gazette* but is best known as the founder of the *Tatler* and co-founder (with Addison) of the *Spectator*. He also owned a cat and a dog which, never having seen other creatures, acquired each other's habits. He described them in the *Tatler* (1711):

> They both of them sit by my fire every Evening and wait with
> Impatience; and, at my entrance, never fail of running up to

me, and bidding me Welcome, each of them in its proper language. As they have been bred up together from infancy, and have seen no other Company, they have acquired each other's Manners; so that the Dog gives himself the Airs of a Cat, and the Cat, in several of her Motions and Gestures, affects the Behaviour of the little Dog.

Gertrude Stein (1874–1946)

US-born writer. When living at 27 Rue de Fleurus, Paris, Stein had a white poodle called Basket (the French children called it Monsieur Basket) which she bought in 1928 at the suggestion of her long-time companion Alice B. Toklas who had wanted one since reading *The Princess Casamassima* by Henry James. The dog was so-called because she thought it looked as if it could carry a basket of flowers in its mouth. Stein disliked Ernest Hemingway and taught the dog to jump and bark when she waved a handkerchief in front of it and said 'Play Hemingway! Be Fierce!'

When it died in 1938 she bought another identical dog, but of German pedigree ('twenty generations are behind him and all of them German') and called him Basket II. However, despite his pedigree, the dog was terrified of Germans during the occupation of France. One day Stein came home with Basket II to discover the house and garden swarming with Nazi troops. The dog was so horrified by the presence of all these uniformed men that he could not even bark in protest, and so she took him up to her bedroom where he just sat and shivered. When the Germans left the next morning Basket II was still in a state of shock and later that day Stein learnt that a dog in the village had been shot for barking and was very worried for her poodle in case he had lost his voice for good. As she recorded in her book *Wars I Have Seen* (1945): 'I am trying to induce him to bark again, it is not right that a dog should be silent.'

Stein and Toklas also had a cat called Hitler which some peasants gave them (the peasants called it thus because of its moustache).

Giles Lytton Strachey (1880–1932)

British writer. Best known for this book *Eminent Victorians* (1918), which included a biography of FLORENCE NIGHTINGALE, Strachey lived in a ménage à trois with DORA CARRINGTON and her husband Ralph Partridge. He was also a friend of MAX BEERBOHM who named one of his cats after him. Strachey himself owned a cat called Tiberius and wrote a poem 'Cat' which begins:

> Dear creature by the fire a-purr,
>> Strange idol, eminently bland,
> Miraculous puss! As o'er your fur
>> I trail a negligible hand,
>
> And gaze into your gazing eyes,
>> And wonder in a demi-dream,
> What mystery it is that lies,
>> Behind those slits that glare and gleam ...

Henry David Thoreau (1817–62)

US writer. The author of *Walden, or Life in the Woods* (1854), which chronicled his life living in a cabin in the woods by Walden Pond, Concord, Massachusetts, from 1845 to 1847, owned a female cat called Min. A great observer of nature and all its creatures, Thoreau remarked in his journal in 1861 about the thin line between the domestic cat and its wild counterpart:

> Only skin deep lies the feral nature of the cat, unchanged still. I just had the misfortune to rock on to our cat's leg, as she was lying playfully spread out under my chair. Imagine the sound that arose, and which was excusable; but what will you say to the fierce growls and flashing eyes with which she met me for a quarter of an hour thereafter? No tiger in its jungle could have been savager.

He also recorded the same year his observations on kittens:

> A kitten is so flexible that she is almost double; the hind parts are equivalent to another kitten with which the fore parts plays. She does not discover that her tail belongs to her till you tread upon it.

The journal entry goes on in similar eloquent prose about the antics of young cats. However, having trodden on his kitten's tail and rocked his chair on to its mother's leg one begins to wonder whether Thoreau was well-suited to own pets ...

Horace Walpole, 4th Earl of Orford
(1717–97)

British writer. Best known for his letters and for such novels as *The Castle of Otranto* (1764) which started a vogue for Gothic romances, Walpole's favourite pet came to an unfortunate end. The tabby cat, Selima, was playing one day with some goldfish in her master's house at Strawberry Hill in London and accidentally fell into the china tub of water they were in and was drowned. But

her memory lives on as her last moments were immortalised by the poet Thomas Gray in his 'On the Death of a Favourite Cat, Drowned in a Tub of Gold Fishes' (1748). Gray describes Selima as 'demurest of the tabby kind', with 'ears of jet, and emerald eyes' as she tries to catch the fish:

> The hapless Nymph with wonder saw:
> A whisker first, and then a claw,
>> With many an ardent wish,
> She stretched in vain to reach the prize.
> What female heart can gold despise?
>> What's Cat's averse to fish?

Alexander Woollcott (1887–1943)

US journalist and broadcaster. Woollcott once famously said, 'All the things I really like to do are either immoral, illegal or fattening.' He also wrote the well-known story of 'Verdun Belle' for *Star and Stripes* about a mongrel dog who followed a US soldier into battle at Château-Thierry. In 1939, when he was living on an island on a lake in Vermont he acquired a white French poodle called Cocaud, named after a Frenchwoman who looked after US troops in the Second World War. It was his third poodle. A pedigree dog from a New York kennel his official name was Blakeen Cerulean. Talking about dogs in a broadcast Woollcott remarked that for many years he had belonged to 'the brotherhood of the poodle', whose members include such disparate figures as the actesses Helen Hayes and Ruth Gordon, and the writers Ben Hecht, GERTRUDE STEIN and BOOTH TARKINGTON. However, one thing that he felt all members of the brotherhood held in common was the belief that 'man, as he walks this earth, can find no more engaging companion than that golden-haired clown, the French poodle'.

Art
&
Fashion

Balthus (1908–2001)

French-born painter. Balthus, whose real name was Count Balthasar Klossowksi de Rola, was best known for his paintings of adolescent girls. He was also a keen cat lover and even drew a self-portrait of himself as *The King of the Cats*. At the age of 13 he produced an album of 40 drawings entitled *Mitsou le Chat* with a preface by the Austrian poet Rainer Maria Rilke (a friend of his mother, Baladine). According to Rilke, when ten years old Balthus found a tomcat at the Château de Nyon and took him home – by boat and tram – to Molard. Here he christened the cat Mitsou and took it for walks on a lead until one day it disappeared.

Balthus only worked in natural daylight and in 1977 he bought the Grand Chalet de Rossiniere, in Switzerland (the biggest chalet in the country) which had formerly been a hotel visited by VICTOR HUGO among others. Here he lived with his Japanese wife Setzuko (30 years his junior) and their daughter Harumi, surrounded by their many cats.

Rosa Bonheur (1822–99)

French painter. Rosa Bonheur was one of Europe's most celebrated animal painters who came to fame with her painting *A Horse Fair* in 1853. She was particularly fond of birds. In addition she had a pet lioness who died in her arms, as she recounted in a letter from 1881:

> I heard a velvet-soft step down in the hall. I went to see what it was, and found that it was my lioness, who, though dying,

had made an effort to see me again for the last time. She knew I had gone upstairs. She heard my voice and had crawled on to the stairs in order to reach me. I went down a little way and she stopped. She lay back and looked at me like a person who thinks, and died thus gazing at me. I believe in the good God and in his Paradise for the just, but I do not approve of everything in religion. For instance, I find it monstrous that animals should be said to have no soul. My lioness loved. She, therefore, had more soul than certain people who do not love.

George Bryan Brummell (1778–1840)
British dandy. 'Beau' Brummell was a fastidious dresser and set the fashions for his day. He was also a close friend of GEORGE IV when Prince Regent until they quarrelled in 1813 and Brummell moved to France in 1816. A great lover of cats, when living in France he owned two females

– Ourika and Angolina. In addition he owned two dogs – Atous and a female terrier Vick – as well as large green macaw, Jacko.

Frank Calderon (1865–1943)

British painter. As well as being a distinguished painter and illustrator himself Frank Calderon was the founder and principal of the School of Animal Painting in Kensington, London (1894–1916) – the only one of its kind in the world – which had many famous pupils. He also lectured on animal anatomy at the Royal Academy Schools and his first picture exhibited at the Royal Academy (*Feeding the Hungry*), at the age of 16, was bought by QUEEN VICTORIA. At one time (*c.* 1901) the school was based at Headly Mill Farm, near Liphook, Hampshire, and some of the models were Calderon's own pets. Among these were a greyhound which appears in his famous picture *The Cavalier's Return*, and an Irish wolfhound called Patrick who featured with two puppies in *Orphans*, the most popular painting Calderon ever showed at the Royal Academy. A very popular model with Calderon's students, after Patrick's death in 1900 a life-sized bronze cast of him was placed in the studio.

Dora Carrington (1893–1932)

British painter. After studying at the Slade School of Art Dora Carrington lived with LYTTON STRACHEY from 1917 and in 1921 married Ralph Partridge. Closely association with the Bloomsbury Group and the circle around

VIRGINIA WOOLF, she had a cat called Tiger in 1929. In April 1922 she wrote a letter to Strachey from The Mill House in Tidmarsh, Pangbourne, Sussex, in which she describes her two cats:

> The black cat in the wildest state of spring lust careers about the garden after Ralph crying out to be raped. Really she is unabashed in her attentions. Old Marmaduke feels the weight of his winter overcoat and rather fretfully lies in the sun on the footpath.

Sir Francis Chantrey (1781–1841)
British sculptor. This famous sculptor owned a Dandie Dinmont terrier called Mustard which was given to him by SIR WALTER SCOTT in return for making a bust of Scott. (Dandie Dinmont was a character in Scott's novel *Guy Mannering* who bred terriers.) Mustard was painted by SIR EDWIN LANDSEER. Chantrey also owned a Pointer dog called Hector and a number of cats.

Ossie Clark (1942–96)
British fashion designer. Ossie Clark (whose real name was Raymond) became famous when he opened his Quorum boutique in London's King's Road, Chelsea, which attracted such celebrity customers as Twiggy and Elizabeth Taylor. When he was murdered in London in 1996 his obituary in the *Daily Telegraph* described him as 'London's answer to Yves Saint Laurent'. A close friend of the painter David Hockney, Ossie Clark and his wife

Celia Birtwell owned a white cat who stars in David Hockney's picture *Mr and Mrs Clark and Percy* (1971), now in the collection of the Tate Gallery, London. In fact the cat's real name was Blanche.

Walt Disney (1901–66)

US animator. During the First World War Disney served in France as a Red Cross van driver and had a dog called Carey, named after the famous Pulitzer Prize-winning US cartoonist of the *Chicago Tribune*, Carey Orr (1890–1967). When working at Newman Laugh-O-Gram Films as a young man in the early 1920s Disney had a pet mouse called Mortimer who was the inspiration for Mickey Mouse. Disney's wife, Lillian, objected to the name Mortimer for the screen version and so it was changed. He later owned a poodle called Lady.

Thomas Gainsborough (1727–88)

British painter. Best known as a landscape painter, for his portraits of royalty and for such works as *The Blue Boy*, Gainsborough also painted his own dogs, Tristram and Fox. Their portrait currently hangs in the Tate Gallery, London.

Dame Barbara Hepworth (1903–75)

British sculptor. A friend of Henry Moore (with whom she studied at Leeds School of Art and the Royal College of Art in London), Hepworth was one of the foremost non-figurative sculptors of her day. After she moved to St Ives in 1939 she had a number of cats including Mimi, Tobey and the black-and-white tom Nicholas.

William Hogarth (1697–1764)

British painter, engraver and caricaturist. Perhaps best known for his series of pictorial satires such as The *Harlot's Progress, The Rake's Progress, Gin Lane and Beer Street*, Hogarth is also generally seen as the father of modern British cartooning. When living in Chiswick, London (now the Hogarth's House museum), he had a pug dog called Trump who features in a famous self-portrait of the artist, *The Painter and His Pug* (1745). When he died the dog was buried in the garden of the house.

It is likely that Hogarth also owned cats as a number appear in his works. Tabbies appear in the *Industrial Apprentice, Hudibras* and other paintings and engravings, and a white cat features in Scene 3 of *The Harlot's Progress*. And the art historian Sir Kenneth Clark (father of ALAN CLARK) was so impressed by the cat in the group portrait *The Graham Children* that he described her as 'the embodiment of cockney vitality, alert and adventurous ... a Nell Gwynne amongst cats', beside which the Graham children looked 'hollow and lifeless'.

Jean Auguste Dominique Ingres (1780–1867)

French painter. As well as painting such famous nudes as *Baigneuse* (1808) Ingres was a professor at the Ecole des Beaux-Arts in Paris and director of the French Academy in Rome. It was here one day that he was preparing to be presented to the Prince Borghese when he received news that his cat Patrocle had died. He cancelled his appointment and spent the rest of the day in mourning.

Gwen John (1876–1939)

British painter. The elder sister of Augustus John, Gwen John's reputation as a painter has grown considerably in recent years. She owned a cat called Valentine that eventually had no teeth and had to be fed calves' liver or cod pâté. In Paris in 1906 she had a female tabby with a white breast called Tiger, who accompanied her wherever she went. On a journey to visit her lover, the French sculptor Auguste Rodin, in Meurdon, Tiger was delighted by her new surroundings and quickly began to inspect the garden as John sketched Rodin's villa: 'It was a pleasure to see the little figure in the country beaming with happiness, her tail straight as she ran.' However, on John's return to Paris Tiger escaped from under her shawl when the tram stopped at St Cloud and disappeared into the night. For nine days she tried to find the animal, sleeping rough in the streets and searching gardens in the area, and later offered a reward of 20 francs for her safe return. Eventually a message came from Meurdon that a cat answering Tiger's description had been seen in the vicinity of Rodin's villa and at 4 a.m. one morning the thin and dirty cat was reunited with her owner.

Paul Klee (1879–1940)

Swiss painter. A member of the 'Blaue Reiter' group and a former teacher at the Bauhaus, Klee owned a number of cats which included Fritzi (a mackerel tabby), Mys, Nuggi and Bimbo (a white long-haired cat).

B. Kliban (1935–90)

US cartoonist. The great US cat cartoonist B. Kliban (his Christian name was in fact Bernard) was unfortunately allergic to cats as a child but later in life got his first moggy, which he named Noko Marie, when living in North Beach, California. He had four cats in all. Noko Marie, a female, had been bought by his wife for three dollars and they kept two of her male offspring – one from her first litter (Norton) and one from her second litter (Nitty). Nitty was Kliban's own favourite. He describes him as a 'big, fat, striped cat'. Some local children then gave his wife a stray cat they called Burton Rustle. The couple became very fond of their four cats and then one day Norton disappeared. As Kliban later recorded: 'It almost broke my heart. Nitty got feline leukaemia and died in my arms – that did break my heart.'

Sir Edwin Landseer (1802–73)

British painter and sculptor. Landseer's best known works include such paintings as *Monarch of the Glen* and the four bronze lions at the foot of Nelson's column in London's Trafalgar Square. A specialist in paintings of dogs and deer, he was also one of QUEEN VICTORIA's favourite artists and painted many of her pets. In fact the art critic JOHN RUSKIN, in a rather cynical aside, once said that: 'It was not by a study of Raphael that he attained his eminent success, but by a healthy love of Scotch Terriers.' Landseer's own dogs, Lassie and Rifa, appear in his self-portrait.

Leonardo da Vinci (1452–1519)

Italian painter and inventor. One of the greatest artistic figures of the Italian Renaissance, Leonardo not only painted such famous works as *The Last Supper* and the *Mona Lisa* but is also credited with numerous inventions such as the helicopter and the parachute. In addition he drew many pictures of cats and even included one in a picture of the infant Jesus called *Madonna and Child with a Cat*. That he was fond of them and may well have kept one as a pet is evidenced in his statement that 'The smallest feline is a masterpiece.'

Sir David Low (1891–1963)

New Zealand-born cartoonist. David Low was the political cartoonist on the *Evening Standard* from 1927 to 1950 and later worked for the *Daily Herald* and *Manchester Guardian*. Apart from his famous political cartoons attacking Hitler and Mussolini during the 1930s and the Second World War, Low is also well-known as the creator of the Coalition Ass, the TUC carthorse and the walrus-moustached old reactionary,

Colonel Blimp. In addition he caused considerable controversy when he introduced the cartoon character Musso the Pup, which was based on his own 'trusty studio companion', whom he had rechristened Mussolini, or Musso for short. However, not everyone appreciated the joke. One day he received a call at the *Evening Standard* office from an excited attaché from the Italian embassy who, as Low recorded in his autobiography, 'conveyed the regrets of the entire Italian people at the desecration of this exalted surname', and demanded that in the interests of international concord the dog should be rechristened.

Phil May (1864–1903)

British cartoonist and illustrator. This famous cartoonist, who was greatly admired by many fine artists, including J.M. WHISTLER (who said of him 'Black-and-white art is summed up in two words – Phil May') was a great lover of horses, having been brought up with them, and at one time wanted to become a jockey. However, unfortunately, May was also a well-known drunk. His work for the *St Stephen's Review* – particularly the illustrations to *The Parson and the Painter* by the *Review's* editor, William Allison – was a great success and enabled him to buy both a house and horse. One day, soon after acquiring the horse, he was en route to the offices of the *Graphic* and dropped into the Savage Club at lunchtime, leaving the horse in the care of a man with instructions to walk him up and down. Meeting up with a jovial crowd, May completely forgot about the horse and later arrived at the *Graphic* on foot. A similar incident happened with his second horse, called Punch, which he left outside the National Sporting Club one day and got so drunk that he took a cab home and forgot all about it till the next day. Nonetheless, despite his forgetfulness, May once said that the horse was his favourite form of transport: 'I much prefer my old gee-gee. He's thrown me off a dozen times, but I have come off without a scratch so far.'

When first married May owned a terrier called Gyp which would keep his wife company when he went off on his long benders. However, Gyp had an unfortunate habit in that he was particularly fond of hats and tore to ribbons any headware – male or female – that was left around the house. After it died May bought his wife another dog, a bulldog which he named Mr Blathers because it was always salivating. They also owned a canary.

Sir Alfred Munnings (1878–1959)

A specialist in painting horses, Munnings was President of the Royal Academy between 1944 and 1949. When a child the family pets included a dog called Friday (which he painted in 1900) and his mother's pony Fanny. However, when still very young Munnings was given his own pony, Merrylegs, which also became his first model after he painted it when he was aged six. In later life Munnings had a 'white, rough-haired mongrel with a black head' called Toby, Welsh terriers Joe and Taffy, and another dog called Bob who was 'a small, quaint, rough-haired, sandy-and-white, self-contained, calm being'.

Norman Pett (1891–1960)

British cartoonist. Norman Pett is best known as the creator of the long-running strip cartoon 'Jane' which was published in the *Daily Mirror*. Jane was originally based on Pett's wife Mary, who in real life had actually received a telegram asking her to look after a distinguished visitor who spoke no English, 'Count Fritz von Pumpernickel', who turned out to be a red dachshund. And this is how the strip began on 5 December 1932. For the next 20 years readers of the *Daily Mirror* followed the adventures of Jane and her dog Fritz which became very popular in the Second World War when Jane used to shed items of clothing in the cartoon and became a pin-up for the troops. Indeed, the US newspaper for forces in the Far East, *Round-up*, ran a wartime headline 'Jane Gives All', and then continued: 'Right smack out of the blue and with no one even threatening her, Jane peeled a week ago. The British 36th Division immediately gained six miles and the British attacked in the Arakan. Maybe we Americans ought to have Jane too.'

Pablo Picasso (1881–1973)

Spanish painter. Born Pablo Blasco (Picasso was his mother's middle name), the famous painter worked in the traditional manner before joining up with Braque to found the Cubist movement in art in 1909. Picasso had an Afghan hound called Kasbec. He also owned a painting made by Congo, a chimpanzee at London Zoo who had been trained by Desmond Morris and whose work was also admired by Dali and Miro.

Beatrix Potter (1866–1943)

British children's book illustrator and writer. Beatrix Potter based many of her children's book characters on animals from her own extensive menagerie which she started as a lonely child with her younger brother Bertram and maintained her whole life long. Along with cats and dogs she kept rabbits, frogs, lizards, pigs and hedgehogs. Her own rabbits Peter Piper and Benjamin Bouncer, which she would walk on leads, appeared on the page as Peter Rabbit and Benjamin Bunny. Other characters, such as Pig-Wig and Mrs Tiggy-Winkle the hedgehog, were also based on real animals – Pig-Wig was her beloved Berkshire sow. The Potter family spent their summers away from London in Scotland and the Lake District and Beatrix would always take her menagerie with her, travelling by train with dogs, rabbits, hedgehogs and other animals packed away in various boxes and hutches. She also bred sheep.

Breton Riviere (1840–1920)

British painter. One of the most famous animal painters of his day, Breton Riviere RA was very fond of all four-footed creatures, especially dogs, sheep and horses which all appeared in his paintings. When living in Kent he had three pigs. When interviewed at his home in Finchley Road, Lodon in 1896 he owned a lively fox-terrier dog called Speed, of which he said:

He never bites anyone except myself and the members of my own family! He bit me a few months ago and one of my sons a few days after, but I have never known him bite a stranger. These are only the eccentricities of genius. He is a dog who thinks, and we are all very fond of him and accept him gladly with these few little failings.

He also owned a number of skeletons of animals including one of the largest leopards ever housed in a zoo and Bevis, a prize-winning deerhound that once belonged to one of his brothers-in-law and which was one of his best models. Of dog models he said:

The best dog to sit is an animal which I am afraid I must admit I thoroughly dislike – an intelligent poodle ... The most restless sitters are the collie and the deerhound ... Perhaps the dog I admire most is the bloodhound; but as a matter of fact, I am fond of all short-haired dogs.

John Ruskin (1819–1900)

British art critic. Among Ruskin's most influential works are *Modern Painters* (1843–60), *The Seven Lamps of Architecture* (1849) and *The Stones of Venice* (1851–53). He was also a great dog-lover and even wrote a poem about his dog Dash in 1880:

I have a dog of Blenheim birth
With fine long ears and full of mirth;
And sometimes, running o'er the plain,
He tumbles on his nose:

But, quickly jumping up again,
Like lightning he goes!

(A Blenheim is a variety of King Charles spaniel.)

Charles Schultz (1922–2000)

US cartoonist. The artist who created the 'Peanuts' strip in 1950 based the character of Charlie Brown on himself and that of Snoopy on the black-and-white dog he had as a child called Spike. When aged 15 Schultz had one of his drawings accepted for the famous 'Ripley's Believe It Or Not' series which featured a picture of Spike illustrating the story 'A hunting dog that eats pins, tacks and razor-blades.' As well as such bizarre items of diet Spike also ate balls and once made himself sick eating too much spaghetti.

Philip Wilson Steer (1860–1942)

British painter. Influenced at first by Impressionism, Steer was the founder of the New English Art Club and taught at the Slade School of Art in London. In his youth he had a tortoiseshell cat called Duchess which was the first subject of his painting in oils. He also owned Mr Pop, Countess and Mr Thomas (who features as a black-and-white kitten in his painting *Hydrangeas* and died in 1906). The second Mr Thomas (featured in *The Muslin Dress*) was an enormous tabby who lived with Steer for 18 years until it died in 1924. Mr Thomas had his own chair and if anyone sat in it the cat would stare at them until Steer pointed out that the seat was already taken and they vacated it. Steer said that he liked the quiet companionship of cats and preferred them because they were not sycophants and provided their own boots. He also kept dogs.

Theophile Steinlen (1859–1923)

Swiss-born painter and graphic artist. Steinlen was probably best known for his book illustrations and his posters, among which were those for the famous Chat Noir (Black Cat) café in Paris which was frequented by many artists and writers of the late 19th century. He was also a great cat lover and not only painted a large number of cats but also cast them in bronze.

James Thurber (1894–1961)

US cartoonist and writer. Thurber had an Airedale dog called Muggs who died at the age of 11. He was so aggressive that Thurber had the words *Cave Canem* (Beware of the Dog) printed on a sign over his grave. He is featured in the story 'The Dog That Bit People' in Thurber's *My Life and Hard Times* (1933):

> Muggs was afraid of only one thing, an electrical storm. Thunder and lightning frightened him out of his senses [...]. He would rush into the house and hide under a bed or in a clothes closet. So we fixed up a thunder machine out of a long narrow piece of sheet iron with a wooden handle on one end. Mother would shake this vigorously when she wanted to get

Muggs into the house. It made an excellent imitation of thunder, but I suppose it was the most roundabout system for running a household that was ever devised. It took a lot out of mother.

Towards the end Muggs started having visions:

A few months before Muggs died, he got to 'seeing things'. He would rise slowly from the floor, growling low, and stalk, stiff-legged and menacing toward nothing at all. Sometimes the Thing would be just a little to the right or left of a visitor. Once a Fuller Brush salesman got hysterics. Muggs came wandering into the room like Hamlet following his father's ghost. His eyes were fixed on a spot just to the left of the Fuller Brush man, who stood it until Muggs was about three slow, creeping paces from him. Then he shouted. Muggs wavered on past him into the hallway grumbling to himself but the Fuller man went on shouting. I think mother had to throw a can of cold water on him before he stopped.

Thurber owned more than 50 dogs in his life, many of which are described in *Thurber's Dogs* (1955). As a child he had an American bull-terrier called Rex that lived ten years:

He had one brindle eye that sometimes made him look like a clown and sometimes reminded you of a politician with derby hat and cigar. The rest of him was white except for a brindle saddle that always seemed to be slipping off and a brindle stocking on a hind leg. Nevertheless there was a nobility about him. He was big and muscular and beautifully made

... We used to bet kids who had never seen Rex in action that he could catch a baseball thrown as high as they could throw it. He almost never let us down. Rex could hold a baseball with ease in his mouth, as if it were a chew of tobacco.

Other dogs included a Scotch terrier and a poodle:

My moment of keenest embarrassment was the time a Scotch terrier named Jeannie, who had just had six puppies in the clothes closet of a fourth floor apartment in New York, had the unexpected seventh and last at the corner of Eleventh Street and Fifth Avenue during a walk she had insisted on taking. Then too, there was the prize-winning French poodle, a great big black poodle – none of your little, untroublesome white miniatures – who got sick riding in the rumble seat of a car with me on her way to the Greenwich Dog Show. She had a red rubber bib tucked around her throat and, since a rainstorm came up when we were halfway through the Bronx, I had to hold over her a small green umbrella, really more of a parasol. The rain beat down fearfully and suddenly the driver of the car drove into a big garage filled with mechanics. It happened so quickly that I forgot to put the umbrella down and I will always remember, with sickening distress, the look of incredulity mixed with hatred that came over the face of the particular hardened garage man that came over to see what we wanted, when he took a look at me and the poodle. All garage men, and people of that intolerant stripe, hate poodles with their curious haircut, especially the pom-poms that you got to leave on their hips if you expect the dogs to win a prize.

Henri de Toulouse-Lautrec (1864–1901)

French painter. Best known for his paintings of the life and society around Paris's Montmartre district, and for his posters for the Moulin Rouge music hall, as a child Toulouse-Lautrec kept a male canary called Lolo.

J.M.W. Turner (1775–1851)

British painter. One of the most important British artists of his day, Turner is famed for such pictures as *The Fighting Temeraire* (1839) and *Rain, Steam and Speed* (1844). He also loved animals and kept five or six dirty-white, pink-eyed tailless cats at his home in Queen Anne Street, London. After his death many of his drawings were found to have paw-prints on them and it is even held that he used an old canvas for a cat flap.

Louis Wain (1860–1939)

British cat artist. Originally trained as a musician, Wain began his professional life as an art teacher and his first published drawing was of bullfinches. However, his life changed when he was given a black-and-white kitten called Peter – later known as 'Peter the Great' – when he was 21, soon after he had married the governess of his younger sisters. His wife had cancer and when she was bedridden the cat was a great comfort to her and Louis began to draw it. Eventually, encouraged by his wife – and against his own better judgement – he sent the drawings of Peter to Sir William Ingram, editor of the *Illustrated London News*, who published them in 1884.

It was thus his pet Peter who inspired his career as a cat artist and who became his principal model and 'pioneer of my success'. As Wain said 'He helped me wipe out, once and for all, the contempt in which the cat had been held in this country.'

This led to numerous other works. However, the first anthropomorphic cats for which Wain is best known did not appear until 1890 and the popular *Louis Wain Annuals* were published from 1901 to 1913. Wain also later became the second President of the National Cat Club and designed the Club's coat of arms and invented its motto: 'Beauty Lives by Kindness'. In addition he produced the first ever animated cartoon cat film, *Pussyfoot*, at Shepperton studios in 1916 (Pat Sullivan's 'Felix the Cat' did not appear until the 1920s).

In 1895 he said that when he was young, no man in the public eye would have dreamed of admitting that he was fond of cats for fear of being looked upon as effeminate, but 'now even MPs can do so without danger of being laughed at'.

Andy Warhol (1927–87)

US pop artist and film-maker. Warhol (real name Andrew Warhola) who was better known for his multiple images of tins of soup and MARILYN MONROE, also produced a series of cat paintings called *25 Cats name [sic] Sam and One Blue Pussy* in the 1950s. His Czech mother Julia Warhola bred Siamese cats when she was living with her son in New York during this period. Warhol's own favourite cat was called Hester.

James Abbott McNeill Whistler (1834–1903)

US painter. Famed for such pictures as *Old Battersea Bridge* and the portrait of his mother, Whistler owned a brown, gold and white cat and a French poodle. One day, when the dog was ill, Whistler summoned a very distinguished throat specialist to look at him. The doctor was outraged that he was called to treat a dog but nonetheless inspected the animal and prescribed some medicine for it. The next day, however, the specialist had his revenge when he sent an urgent message to the famous painter to come to his house. Thinking the summons had to do with his beloved dog, Whistler quickly went round to the house where he was greeted by the doctor with the words: 'Good morning, Mr Whistler. I wanted to see you about painting my front door.'

Miscellaneous

Jeremy Bentham (1748–1832)

British philosopher, jurist and social reformer. Bentham is perhaps best remembered as the proponent of 'utilitarianism' which argues that the object of all conduct should be 'the greatest happiness of the greatest number'. When living at Queen Square Place in London Bentham had a cat called Sir John Langbourne which ate macaroni. A frisky cat in his youth, as he grew older he became increasingly sedate and thoughtful and took to going to church. This decided Bentham that the cat should lay down his title and become the Rev. John Langbourne and as his reputation for learning and sanctity grew he conferred on him a doctorate. When he died, Bentham said, the general opinion was that he was 'not far off a mitre'. The sacred body was buried in a cemetery in the garden in Bentham's house which had once been owned by Milton. Bentham also liked mice and encouraged them to come into his house.

Tycho Brahe (1546–1601)

Danish astronomer. One of the greatest astronomers of the Renaissance, Brahe discovered a new star in the constellation of Cassiopaea, founded the world's first major observatory and was royal astrologer and almanac-maker to the Danish royal family. His great pupil was Kepler who built on his work to reject the geocentric theory of the universe in favour of the Copernican (sun-centred) theory. Brahe owned a pet elk which he sent one day to the Landgrave of Hesse-Cassel (his patron) but on the way it somehow managed to drink a bucket full of beer and fell down some stairs, broke a leg and died.

Baroness Burdett-Coutts (1814–1906)

British philanthropist. The daughter of Sir Francis Burdett and granddaughter of the banker Thomas Coutts, she inherited her grandfather's fortune in 1837 and at the age of 23 was the richest woman in Britain. She spent the money on good works, and was an active promoter of the Society for the Prevention of Cruelty to Animals as well as its President. She received a peerage in 1872 and became the first women to be given the Freedom of the City of London in 1872. When interviewed at her house, Holly Lodge in Highgate, in 1894 she had a number of dogs (including her favourites Peter

and Prince and one whose father was the favourite dog of Emperor Charles Frederick), a white donkey, goats (including Sir Garnet who was painted by Edmund Caldwell), cows, horses, pigs and fowls. She even wrote a biography of her Manchester terrier, Fan.

In addition she kept in her house a cockatoo called Cocky, who was also painted by Edmund Caldwell. Cocky and the three main dogs were drawn as a cartoon by Caldwell for the baroness's Christmas card in 1892. She was also a keen beekeeper (she was President of the Bee Society) and once kept llamas but they died and she had two of them stuffed.

It was through her efforts that the famous statue to the Skye terrier, Greyfriars Bobby, was erected in Edinburgh in 1872.

Richard Byrd (1888–1957)
US explorer. Rear-Admiral Richard Byrd was the navigator on the first-ever aeroplane flight over the North Pole in 1926 and also organised a number of expeditions to the South Pole. He owned a smooth-haired white fox-terrier called Igloo who often accompanied him on his travels. More familiarly known as Iggy, the dog was with Byrd on his first Antarctic expedition and even had his biography written by Jane Brevoort Walden in 1931. When he died he was buried in the Pine Ridge Cemetery for Small Animals in Dedham, Massachusetts. The triangular stone has the inscription: 'Igloo. He was more than a friend.'

John Cobb (1899–1952)

British racing champion. The Scotsman John Cobb was the first person in the world to travel at more than 350 mph on land. He achieved the world land speed record on 15 September 1938 driving his Napier-Railton Mobil Special car on Bonneville Salt Flats, Utah, USA. Just before setting off to the USA to break the record, two kittens were born in the cockpit of his car. He named them Inlet and Exhaust. (Cobb broke the record again in 1939 and in 1947 before he was killed on Loch Ness, Scotland, after breaking another world speed record, becoming the first man to travel at 200 mph on water.)

Charles Darwin (1809–82)

British naturalist. Darwin was the grandson of the physician ERASMUS DARWIN. His book *On the Origin of Species* (1859) introduced his famous theory of evolution, based on natural selection, and his views were further expounded in *The Descent of Man* (1871) which applied his theory to human beings. Darwin's dog Bob featured in his book *The Expression of the Emotions in Man and Animals* (1872). The great naturalist also kept more than 10,000 barnacles in his house which he studied for a period of eight years (his first published book was a monograph on barnacles) and he was a keen coleopterist (student of beetles). As a young man he was very fond of dogs and his father once told him: 'You care for nothing but shooting, dogs and rat-catching, and you will be a disgrace to yourself and all your family.'

Erasmus Darwin (1731–1808)

British physician, poet and hymn-writer. The grand-father of CHARLES DARWIN owned a white cat called Persian Snow when he lived in the old vicarage in Lichfield, Staffordshire. A neighbour was the poet Anna Seward (1747–1809), the 'Swan of Lichfield', who also owned a cat, Po Felina, and the two exchanged letters written as if from their cats to each other. These were published in Seward's biography of Darwin. At the end of Persian Snow's love-letter dated 7 September 1780 the tom cat offers Po Felina new milk 'in flowing abundance, and mice pent up in twenty garrets, for your food and amusement' and, having just caught a huge rat for her, continues with a poem:

> Cats I scorn, who sleek and fat.
> Shiver at a Norway rat;
> Rough and hardy, bold and free,
> Be the cat that's made for me!
> He, whose nervous paws can take
> My lady's lapdog by the neck;
> With furious hiss attack the hen,
> And snatch a chicken from the pen.
> If the treacherous swain should prove
> Rebellious to my tender love,
> My scorn the vengeful paw shall dart,
> Shall tear his fur, and pierce his heart.

Not surprisingly, Po Felina turns the beast down with another poem and a letter which begins:

I am too sensible of the charms of Mr Snow; but while I
admire the spotless whiteness of his ermine, and the tyger-
strength of his commanding form, I sigh in secret, that he,
who sucked the milk of benevolence and philosophy, should
yet retain the extreme of that fierceness, too justly imputed
to the grimalkin race.

Darwin also said that 'To respect a cat is the beginning
of the aesthetic sense.'

René Descartes (1596–1650)

French philosopher and mathematician. The great
philosopher who coined the phrase 'Cogito, ergo sum' ('I
think, therefore I am') also believed that animals do not
have souls. Nonetheless, at the age of 48 when he was living in Holland, he had a dog called Monsieur Grat.

Gerald Durrell (1925–95)

British naturalist. Durrell owned a number of animals
and describes the dogs of his childhood in *My Family and
Other Animals,* the account of his family's time spent on
the island of Corfu. Every evening his mother would take
their dogs for a walk and the family would watch with
great amusement as they went down the local hillside.
The procession would be led by Roger, the 'senior dog',
followed by two more dogs with the endearing names of
Puke and Widdle. Then would come his mother, who
always wore a huge straw hat on such outings, which to
Durrell made her look like 'an animated mushroom'.

Following his mother would come the oldest dog Dodo, gasping and waddling, and last of all would be Sophia 'carrying the imperial puppy on its cushion.'

In addition to Roger and the other dogs, the young Gerald maintained a menagerie of local wildlife which included a kicking donkey, geckos, toads, scorpions, bats and butterflies. His family became so sick of the chaos his pets caused running rampant through the house that he was given a special room in which to store his animals.

From his earliest years it had been Durrell's ambition to run his very own zoo – his mother claimed 'zoo' was his very first word – and after years collecting rare and endangered breeds from Africa and South America for British zoos, Durrell started collecting animals for his own zoo which he set up in Jersey, a task he described in *Menagerie Manor* (1964).

Benjamin Franklin (1706–90)

US scientist and statesman. Franklin was one of the major figures involved in the drafting of the US Declaration of Independence and among his many other achievements was the invention of the lightning conductor. For many years Franklin tried to woo the Parisian Madame Helvétius who kept 18 cats that only dined on breast of chicken. He even wrote her a spoof petition as if written by her cats, 'An Humble Petition Presented to Madame Helvétius by her Cats':

> We shall not endeavour to defend ourselves equally from devouring as many sparrows, blackbirds, and thrushes, as we can possibly catch. But here we have to plead in extenuation, that our most cruel enemies, your Abbés themselves, are incessantly complaining of the ravages made by these birds among the cherries and other fruit. [...]
>
> We know that we are also accused of eating nightingales, who never plunder, and sing, as they say, most enchantingly. It is indeed possible that we may now and then have gratified our palates with a delicious morsel in this way, but we can assure you that it was in utter ignorance of your affection for the species; and that, resembling sparrows in their plumage, we, who make no pretensions to being connoisseurs in music, could not distinguish the song of the one from that of the other, and therefore supposed ourselves regaling only on sparrows.

Sigmund Freud (1856–1939)

Austrian-born psychiatrist. The great psychoanalyst became very fond of dogs in his old age, keeping an Alsatian called Wolf at the age of 70. In 1928 he was given a chow by the name of Lun-Yu, which unfortunately got run over. Another chow, Jo-fi, which he owned for seven years, used to sleep in a corner during his analysis sessions and always got up and stretched when the patient's hour was up. According to the psychologist Dr Stanley Coren, Freud often used the dog to assess the initial state of mind of his patients. If a patient was tense the dog would lie down on the far side of the room but if they were calm Jo-Fi would lie down much closer to them.

Freud was also a friend of PRINCESS MARIE BONAPARTE (granddaughter of NAPOLEON's brother Lucien) and translated her book about her chow Topsy from French into German,

St Jerome (*c.* AD 342–420)

Christian ascetic and scholar. St Jerome, whose original name was Eusebius Hieronymous, came from Croatia and is best known for making the first ever translation of the Bible from Hebrew into Latin (the Vulgate). However he is also well known for his fondness for cats. As an old children's poem has it:

> If I lost my little cat, I should be sad without it,
> I should ask St Jerome what to do about it,
> I should ask St Jerome, just because of that
> He's the only saint I know that kept a pussy-cat.

William Laud (1573–1645)

Archbishop of Canterbury. This famous clergyman, whose attempt to anglicise the church in Scotland led to the Bishops' Wars and eventually his execution, also owned one of the first tabby cats, which were introduced into Britain in the 1630s. (The original Old English cats were blue-black and white.)

Pope Leo XII (1760–1829)

Head of the Roman Catholic Church. Pope Leo XII (Annibale della Genga) was one of three popes who are recorded as having owned cats, the other two being Gregory XV and PIUS IX. Leo's cat Micetto – a large grey-and-red cat banded with black – was born in the loggia of Raphael in the Vatican itself and would always sit on a fold of the Pope's white robe when he granted ambassadorial audiences. Micetto was accustomed to taking his daily promenade high up in the dome of St Angelo. On Leo's death in 1829 the cat was bequeathed to one of his most ardent admirers, the French writer/diplomat VICOMTE DE CHATEAUBRIAND who was ambassador in Rome.

Charles Lindbergh (1902–74)

US aviator. Lindbergh had a black cat called Patsy with whom he was photographed in the cockpit of his plane *Spirit of St Louis* just before taking off to make his historic first ever non-stop solo flight from New York to Paris in 1927. Asked if he would be taking Patsy along with him Lindbergh replied: 'It's too dangerous a journey to risk the cat's life.' The cat also later featured with Lindbergh on a Spanish postage stamp issued on 10 October 1930 as one of a series of eight stamps honouring famous aviators. This was the first time that a domestic cat had ever featured on a postage stamp and Patsy can be seen in the bottom right-hand corner looking on as Lindbergh's plane flies past the Statue of Liberty en route to Europe while a portrait of Lindbergh himself occupies the left of the picture.

Lindbergh also owned a number of dogs. After he retired from aviation he travelled the world in the cause of conservation and was particularly drawn to the Hawaiian island of Maui where his friend Samuel Pryor lived with three pet gibbons. So attached did Lindbergh become to Pryor's three gibbons that, having been refused permission to be buried in his local pet cemetery in the USA along with his dogs, he asked to be interred on a hillside in Maui between the three monkeys and his own last dog. Despite initial objections from the local authorities his request was finally granted.

Konrad Lorenz (1903–89)

Austrian Zoologist. Lorenz, who was awarded the Nobel Prize for Physiology or Medicine in 1973, was perhaps best known for his books *King Solomon's Ring* (1949) and *Man Meets Dog* (1950). He had an Alsatian and Chow crossbred dog called Stasi who is described in his book *Man Meets Dog*. He also had an Alsatian bitch called Tito and his wife had a chow bitch called Pygi.

Mohammed (AD 570–632)

Founder of Islam. Mohammed apparently did not like dogs which he considered unclean. However, he did have a cat called Muezza. One day the cat was sleeping on his sleeve when the prophet wanted to get up to pray and rather than disturb him he cut off the sleeve. Later Mohammed assigned a place in paradise for the cat and stroked the cat's back three times to give it nine lives and the ability to land on its feet after a fall. The 'M' pattern on tabby cats' foreheads has been ascribed to Mohammed's love of the animals (another story has it that a cat came into the stable after the birth of Jesus and that where Mary pushed it gently away the mark was formed). One of Mohammed's disciples, Abuherrira, was also fond of cats and features in Goethe's poem 'The Favoured Beasts':

> Abuherrira's cat, too, is here
> Purrs round his master blest,
> For holy must the beast appear
> The Prophet hath caress'd.

Michel de Montaigne (1533–92)

French philosopher and essayist. Montaigne had a cat called Madame Vanity who is described in his *Essays*, II, 12 (1580). He famously said of her:

> When my cat and I entertain each other with mutual apish tricks, as playing with a garter, who knows but that I make my cat more sport than she makes me? Shall I conclude her

to be simple, that has her time to begin or refuse to play as freely as I myself have? Nay, who knows but that it is a defect of my not understanding her language (for doubtless cats talk and reason with one another) that we agree no better? And who knows but that she pities me for being no wiser than to play with her, and laughs and censures my folly for making sport for her, when we two play together?

Sir Isaac Newton (1642–1727)

British astronomer and mathematician. Newton alleged-ly had a dog called Diamond which led to his nervous breakdown at Trinity College in 1693. The legend has it that Newton returned from chapel one morning to dis-cover that the dog had knocked over a candle and burnt all his scientific notes. However, though there was a fire in 1683, no major damage was done and there seems to be no evidence for the incident and no proof of the exis-tence of the dog. Newton also kept cats and it was for the cat at Woolsthorpe House that he is reputed to have invented the cat flap.

Florence Nightingale (1820–1910)

British pioneer nurse. 'The Lady of the Lamp', who saved so many lives during the Crimean War, reputedly kept 60 Persian cats (including Bismarck, Disraeli and Gladstone) and always had two or three in her room. In 1890 she wrote to a friend:

I learnt the lesson of life from a little kitten of mine, one of two. The old cat comes in and says, very cross, 'I didn't ask you in here, I like to have my Missus to myself!' And he runs at them. The bigger and handsome kitten runs away, but the littler one *stands her ground*, and when the old enemy comes near enough kisses his nose, and makes the peace. That is the lesson of life, to kiss one's enemy's nose, always standing one's ground.

Another pet was a small owl which she took everywhere in her pocket (even in the Crimea). Nightingale felt that animals also had health benefits and in her book *Notes on Nursing* (1859) said: 'A small pet is often an excellent companion for the sick, for long chronic cases especially.'

Pope Pius IX (1846–78)

Head of the Roman Catholic Church. Pope Pius IX (Giovanni Maria Mastai Ferretti) allegedly had a cat which would patiently sit waiting for him to finish his dinner before being served his own food, at the Pope's table. Though why Pius did not feed the cat first is not clear!

Cardinal Richelieu (1585–1642)

French priest and statesman. LOUIS XIII's chief minister, virtual dictator of France and one of the most powerful and feared statesmen of the 17th century, Armand Jean du Plessis – the iron-willed Cardinal Richelieu – was simply potty about cats. He may have crushed France's European rivals, the Habsburgs, and cruelly suppressed the Huguenots in his own country, but at home his 14 cats walked all over him – literally. Wherever he went in his palace in Paris at least a dozen cats would follow and two attendants were hired exclusively to look after their needs. He was particularly fond of kittens and his favourite cat was Soumise, who often slept on his lap. Others included Gazette, Rita, Rubis, Pyramus, Thisbe, Serpolet, jet-black Lucifer and the rat-torturing Ludovic the Cruel. Richelieu was also a considerable patron of the arts, wrote plays himself and even founded the prestigious Academie Français in 1635. So perhaps it is not surprising that he named two more of his cats after one of the original members of this august assembly. Racan and Perruque were so-called because they were born in the academician's wig (*perruque*) which the absent-minded

Marquis de Racan (a poet) had left lying about and their mother had adopted as a nest! Richelieu's kindness to his cats even continued after his death as each one of his pets – as well as their attendants – was left a sizeable pension in his will.

Jean-Jacques Rousseau (1712–78)

French philosopher. Rousseau's masterpiece was *The Social Contract* (1762) which had a great influence on the French Revolution and introduced the phrase 'Liberty, Equality, Fraternity'. He owned a number of dogs including Duke (later renamed Turk) and Sultan (a small brown dog with short ears and a short curled tail). It is also fair to assume that Rousseau owned a cat for he once wrote: 'Watch a cat when it enters a room for the first time. It searches and smells about, it is not quiet for a moment, it trusts nothing until it has examined and made acquaintance with everything.'

Jean-Paul Sartre (1905–80)

French philosopher. The author of *Being and Nothingness* and the 'Paths of Freedom' trilogy of novels was evidently not a great dog-lover, for he wrote in his autobiography *Words* (1964), 'Liking children and dogs too much is a substitution for loving adults.' However, he did own a black-and-white cat.

Arthur Schopenhauer (1788–1860)

German philosopher. Best known for his book *The World as Will and Idea* (1819), Schopenhauer's work greatly influenced Existentialism. He enjoyed riding and kept a poodle called Atma ('world-soul').

Albert Schweitzer (1875–1965)

Alsatian medical missionary. Schweitzer won the Nobel Peace Prize in 1952 and owned a number of animals which are described in his book *The Animal World of Albert Schweitzer* (1950). Among these was a tame wild boar called Josephine which he bought in Africa and which would attend church services. Eventually it started killing hens and was slaughtered. Another pet when Schweitzer was working in Africa as a missionary doctor was Sizi the cat. Sizi liked to fall asleep on Schweitzer's left arm and the story goes that, rather than disturb the cat, Schweitzer – who was left-handed – would write prescriptions with his right hand. Schweitzer once said: 'There are two means of refuge from the miseries of life: music and cats.'

Sir Peter Scott (1909–89)

British naturalist and painter. Scott kept a number of animals throughout his life – childhood pets including owls, bats, a Spiny Lizard called Zonure and an Eyed Lizard called Moctaques, which he caught near the mouth of the Loire River in France when on holiday on the island of Noirmoutier. From 1933 to 1939 he lived in an 18th-century lighthouse – East Lighthouse, Sutton Bridge, Lincolnshire – where he kept 200 tame waterfowl, including 25 different types of geese, and once told the journalist PAUL GALLICO about a wild pink-footed goose which came there two years running and which he named Anabel. The story later became the basis for Gallico's bestseller, *The Snow Goose*, which Scott illustrated. Scott also owned a

Shetland collie dog called Piper in 1960 and a Blue Merle Collie called Spookie which features in his painting *Peter and Philippa with Some of Their Favourite Animals* (1982).

Robert Falcon Scott (1868–1912)

British explorer. Scott took an Aberdeen terrier called Scamp with him when he commanded the National Antarctic Expedition (1901–04) which discovered King Edward VII Land. And on his last fateful expedition to the Antarctic – the Terra Nova Expedition (1910–13) in which he and all the members of his team died after reaching the South Pole only to find a Norwegian expedition under Amundsen had beaten them to it by a month – his shipboard companion was a black cat called Nigger.

Captain Oates insisted that the cat should be left on board the ship when they set off for the last dash to the Pole but before they did so it was unfortunately washed overboard by a freak wave and drowned.

Jonathan Swift (1667–1745)

Irish writer and clergyman. Swift is best known for his famous satire, *Gulliver's Travels* (1726). He seems to have been at least tolerant of dogs for he once wrote an inscription for the collar of Mrs Dingley's lap-dog Tiger which read:

> Pray steal me not; I'm Mrs Dingley's,
> Whose heart in this four-footed thing lies.

He also wrote a poem entitled 'The Cat and the Rain':

> Careful observers may foretell the hour
> (By sure prognostics) when to dread a shower;
> While rain depends, the pensive cat gives o'er
> Her frolics, and pursues her tail no more.

Hippolyte Taine (1828–93)

French critic, historian and philosopher. Perhaps best known for this book *The Origins of Contemporary France*, which attacked the French Revolution, Taine also wrote poetry, including 12 sonnets to his three cats: Puss, Ebène and Mitonne.

Dick Turpin (1705–39)

British highwayman. The Essex-born Richard Turpin, who was hanged in York in 1739, had a famous mare called Black Bess which features in the highly successful romanticised account of his life by Harrison Ainsworth, *Rookwood* (1834). In the novel Turpin rides 180 miles from London to York on Black Bess.

A.N. Whitehead (1861–1947)

British philosopher and mathematician. Whitehead is perhaps best remembered for his collaboration with his former pupil, Bertrand Russell, on the book *Principia Mathematica*. However, he must also have owned at least one cat and dog for he once observed: 'If a dog jumps into your lap, it is because he is fond of you; but if a cat does the same thing, it is because your lap is warmer.'

Acknowledgements

Max Beerbohm, from Michael Holroyd, *Lytton Strachey: A Critical Biography* (Heinemann, 1967), reprinted by kind permission of Random House and A.P. Watt Ltd on behalf of Michael Holroyd. John Galsworthy, from *The Inn of Tranquillity* (Heinemann 1912), reprinted by kind permission of the Estate of John Galsworthy and Christopher Sinclair-Stevenson. Aldous Huxley, from *The Collected Works of Aldous Huxley* (Chatto & Windus, 1970), reprinted by kind permission of Random House and the Reece Halsey Agency. James Thurber, from *My Life and Hard Times* (Hamish Hamilton, 1950), copyright Rosemary A Thurber, reprinted by kind permission of Rosemary A Thurber and the Barbara Hogenson Agency. Sylvia Townsend Warner from Claire Harman, *Sylvia Townsend Warner: A Biography* (Chatto & Windus, 1989), reprinted by kind permission of Random House

Every effort has been made to contact copyright-holders. However the author and publishers would be pleased to hear from any that they have been unable to trace and due acknowledgement will be made in future editions.